S0-AHH-055

Prima's Official Strategy Guide

David Ellis

Prima Games
A Division of Random House, Inc.
3000 Lava Ridge Court
Roseville, CA 95661
(800) 733-3000
www.primagames.com

The Prima Games logo is a registered trademark of Random House, Inc., registered in the United States and other countries. Primagames.com is a registered trademark of Random House, Inc., registered in the United States.

© 2003 by Prima Games. All rights reserved. No part of this book may be reproduced or transmitted in any form or by any means, electronic or mechanical, including photocopying, recording, or by any information storage or retrieval system without written permission from Prima Games. Prima Games is a division of Random House, Inc.

Product Manager: Sara Wilson
Senior Project Editor: Brooke N. Hall
Editorial Assistant: Tamar D. Foster
Design & Layout: Bryan Neff, Damon Carlson, Jody Seltzer

Unreal® II–The Awakening© 2003 Epic Games Inc. Raleigh, N.C. USA Unreal and the Unreal logo are registered trademarks of Epic Games, Inc. ALL RIGHTS RESERVED. Unreal II–The Awakening was created by Legend Entertainment, an Infogrames studio and was manufactured and marketed by Infogrames, Inc. New York, NY under license from Epic Games, Inc. The Atari trademark and logo are the property of Infogrames. All other trademarks are the property of their respective owners.

All products and characters mentioned in this book are trademarks of their respective companies.

Please be advised that the ESRB rating icons, "EC", "K-A", "E", "T", "M", "AO" and "RP" are copyrighted works and certification marks owned by the Interactive Digital Software Association and the Entertainment Software Rating Board and may only be used with their permission and authority. Under no circumstances may the rating icons be self-applied or used in connection with any product that has not been rated by the ESRB. For information regarding whether a product has been rated by the ESRB, please call the ESRB at 1-800-771-3772 or visit www.esrb.org. For information regarding licensing issues, please call the IDSA at (212) 223-8936. Please note that ESRB ratings only apply to the content of the game itself and does NOT apply to the content of this book.

Important:
Prima Games has made every effort to determine that the information contained in this book is accurate. However, the publisher makes no warranty, either expressed or implied, as to the accuracy, effectiveness, or completeness of the material in this book; nor does the publisher assume liability for damages, either incidental or consequential, that may result from using the information in this book. The publisher cannot provide information regarding game play, hints and strategies, or problems with hardware or software. Questions should be directed to the support numbers provided by the game and device manufacturers in their documentation. Some game tricks require precise timing and may require repeated attempts before the desired result is achieved.

ISBN: 0-7615-3967-0
Library of Congress Catalog Card Number: 2002117602
Printed in the United States of America

03 04 05 06 DD 10 9 8 7 6 5 4 3 2 1

Dedication
To Meghan, my wife, and our 10+ happy years together.

Acknowledgments
There are lots of people to thank this time around. First, I want to thank the folks at Epic Games, Infogrames, and Legend—especially Mark Rein and Aron Drayer—for getting me the builds and info I needed when I needed them. I also want to thank everyone at Prima Games: Thanks to Jill Hinkley and Jennifer Crotteau for giving me the opportunity to write this book, and to Brooke Hall and Tamar Foster for making the editing process smooth and painless.

And, as always, thanks to my wife Meghan for believing in me and encouraging me to live my dream.

Contents

Chapter 1: Introduction

FROM: CIC TERRAN COLONIAL AUTHORITY

TO: DALTON, JOHN—TCA MARSHAL

Welcome to the ranks of the Terran Colonial Authority, Dalton. You're about to embark on an operation that is more strenuous and challenging than anyone realizes. Luckily, with this training manual in hand, you have the skills necessary to complete the assignment.

Welcome to *Unreal II–The Awakening*

Stationed on the edge of known space, you are John Dalton, a marshal in the Terran Colonial Authority (TCA). You and the crew of your ship, the *Atlantis* might have been expecting an easy assignment, but you're in for a surprise. With every mission, you uncover a new piece of an ancient mystery that's got every hostile corporation and species in the quadrant up in arms.

How to Use This Book

This official guide to *Unreal II–The Awakening* is divided into two sections for easy reference. The first part introduces you to the basic game concepts, equipment, and characters:

- **Chapter 2** looks at the basics of getting around in *Unreal II*. The game mechanics and interface are covered, as well as the basic techniques of moving through and interacting with the game environment.

- **Chapter 3** takes you into *Unreal II*'s arsenal, and introduces you to the weapons and equipment used in the game. Learn the strengths and weaknesses of every weapon so that you know which one to use in any situation.

- **Chapter 4** introduces you to the characters with whom you interact. This chapter provides background info on your allies and the strengths and weaknesses of your enemies.

The second part of the book takes you through the game. Starting with Chapter 5, there's a step-by-step walkthrough for every mission, filled with hints, tips, and tricks to guide you through the mission and allow you to survive every situation.

Caution

The mission walkthroughs in Chapters 5–18 contain spoilers that reveal elements of the game's story. If you don't want to know what's coming next, read only as far as the mission you are currently playing.

Part I: Pre-Mission Training

It's never a good idea to go out in the field without being properly prepared, and it wouldn't do to send a raw recruit out to face the Skaarj without first knowing the basics.

Part I of this guide provides you with a course on the controls and movement modes in *Unreal II*. The chapters also brief you on your available weapons and equipment, introduce you to the allies you're working with, and the enemies against whom you're fighting.

Chapter 2: Basic Skills

Before you dive into your role as a TCA marshal, you should know the basic skills you need to survive. *Unreal II–The Awakening* requires more than just a quick trigger finger. You need dexterity and skill to move around in and manipulate your environment and avoid injury. You also need to know what to do when your physical condition becomes critical on a mission.

This chapter has info you need to move like a pro, including suggestions for control customization. It also introduces you to the concepts of shields and health, and explains the game's save and load system—your best insurance against an unexpected demise.

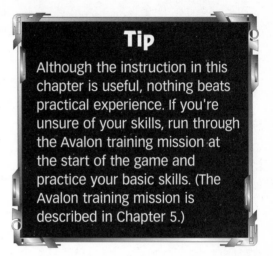

Tip

Although the instruction in this chapter is useful, nothing beats practical experience. If you're unsure of your skills, run through the Avalon training mission at the start of the game and practice your basic skills. (The Avalon training mission is described in Chapter 5.)

Getting Around

You need more than steady aim and a mastery of weapons to survive in *Unreal II*—you must be able to effectively navigate and interact with your environment. Doing so requires the mastery of a variety of movement skills.

Walking and Running

Running is your default movement mode in *Unreal II*. You need to move quickly in most situations. You can, however, switch to a slower walking mode whenever you choose. (By default, holding down `shift` while moving makes you to walk instead of run.)

The only time you should walk is when you move through an area where haste could cause a fatal misstep (see figure 2-1). Examples include moving near the edge of a steep drop or traversing narrow catwalks or ledges above poisonous or otherwise deadly substances.

Fig. 2-1. **Walk in a situation where a misstep can cause serious injury or death.**

Note

You climb some impressive slopes in *Unreal II*. Usually, you can walk up most ramps, columns, or hills as long as their slopes are (roughly) 60 degrees or less. Use this ability to get above your enemies and gain a good vantage point from which to fight (see figure 2-2).

Fig. 2-2. **Run up angled surfaces to get a bird's-eye view of your targets.**

Swimming

There aren't many swimming holes in *Unreal II*, but occasionally you must traverse a liquid environment to search for equipment or to get from place to place (see figure 2-3). Luckily, your armor protects you in aquatic environments—most notably by providing you with an unlimited supply of air. You can stay underwater as long as you want without suffering ill effects.

Swimming is almost identical to walking. The only difference is that the Jump control causes you to rise to the surface.

Fig. 2-3. Sometimes swimming is the only way to get where you're going.

Caution

Not all liquid is water! Unless you're sure the rippling surface you're about to leap into is harmless, avoid it, or test it by stepping in where you can get out if you start taking damage.

Jumping

Not all mission sites are easy to navigate. When you come to a rift that is too wide to step over or a ledge that is too high to step onto, jumping is your only alternative (see figure 2-4).

Fig. 2-4. Precision jumping is sometimes the only way to navigate through treacherous environments.

To jump over an open space, get a running start and press the Jump control when you're near the edge of the obstacle you're trying to clear. The amount of running start you need depends on the distance you need to jump and the size of the landing area, so (literally) look before you leap. Too much speed can cause you to overshoot the landing area.

To climb onto a ledge or similar obstacle (a task known as "mantling"), press and hold the Jump control when you're in front of the ledge you want to climb onto. If mantling doesn't work, the object you're attempting to climb onto is too high to reach.

Caution

When contemplating a jump from a high area to a lower one, assess the situation first to see if you can drop from your current position onto the one below. In some cases, jumping over the edge adds enough height to your fall to cause injury in a situation where a drop is harmless.

Crouching

Crouching serves two purposes. First, it allows you to navigate under obstacles and move through crawl-spaces (see figure 2-5).

Crouching also helps you avoid enemy fire. Most battles take place in areas with ample natural or manmade cover. When your enemies are using ranged attacks, crouch down behind cover to avoid incoming fire.

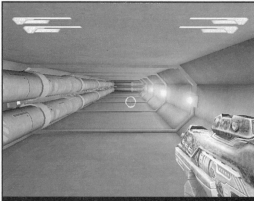
Fig. 2-5. Crouching allows you to enter and move through areas that are too small to allow upright passage.

Leaning

Leaning lets you peek out from behind cover and survey an area without presenting a full-size target to your enemies (see figure 2-6). Use leaning in combination with crouching for maximum cover in dangerous areas.

Fig. 2-6. Leaning around a corner lets you check out a new area without fully exposing yourself.

"Using"

Throughout the game, you encounter objects—usually hatches, doors, switches, and the like—that you must manipulate in order to move through an area or complete mission objectives. The Use control lets you interact with these objects. When you encounter a "usable" object, a bracket appears around the object when you are close enough to manipulate it (see figure 2-7).

Fig. 2-7. Objects that you can interact with highlight when you are close enough to "use" them.

The Use control also lets you initiate conversations with certain characters. When you approach a person you can talk to, brackets identical to those that appear around usable objects ("use recticles") appear around the person. Press the Use control to initiate a conversation.

Mission Objectives

More often than not, your objectives at the start of a mission are only the tip of the iceberg. As you progress, additional mission objectives are often added. Whenever a new objective is added, you are notified by an on-screen message. To see the new objective—or to review your objectives at any time—press F4.

Customizing the Controls

Every game control for moving, shooting, changing weapons, and all other tasks in *Unreal II* is pre-programmed, or "mapped," to a set of default controls on the keyboard and mouse (or joystick). These controls are customizable, and you can map them to any key or button you prefer from the game's Options menu.

Every experienced first-person shooter player seems to have his or her favorite control mapping system. If you haven't developed a system of your own, check out Table 2-1 for mapping suggestions for some of the major movement and combat controls. The custom mapping shown in the table clusters most of the major controls on the mouse and around the cursor keys on the keyboard, making it easy to play without looking away from the action.

Table 2-1. Custom Control Mapping Suggestions

Control	Suggested Mapping
Move Forward	↑
Move Backward	↓
Strafe Left	←
Strafe Right	→
Jump	shift
Crouch	ctrl
Lean Left	,
Lean Right	.

Control	Suggested Mapping
Use	MiddleMouse or $\boxed{enter}$ *
Primary Fire	Left Mouse
Alternate Fire	Right Mouse
Reload	$\boxed{R}$
Previous Weapon	Mousewheel Up or $\boxed{[}$
Next Weapon	Mousewheel Down or $\boxed{]}$

* MiddleMouse refers to pressing the mousewheel down on a mouse that is aptly equipped.

Note

When you custom map a control to a key or button that was already used in the default control-mapping scheme, remap that control to another key or button.

Saving and Loading

Unreal II lets you save your game at any time. Use this feature frequently to avoid starting over at the beginning of a mission after an untimely death. Save the game using the Save option on the Main Menu, or hit the QuickSave control ($\boxed{F5}$ by default).

Note

There are only 10 save game slots available, two of which are reserved for QuickSaves. You must overwrite previous saves if you want to save additional games. QuickSaves automatically overwrite one another if there is no empty QuickSave slot.

Load a game by selecting it from the Load menu. Games are listed by mission name and section. (The mission descriptions in Chapters 5–18 are divided into sections corresponding to names of the mission sections as they appear on the Load menu.) Mousing over a save name shows the time and date that the save was created. You also can use the QuickLoad command ($\boxed{F8}$ by default) to load the most recent QuickSave.

After you play the first mission, an additional option becomes available on the Load menu—Missions. As you complete each mission and cutscene in *Unreal II*, the completed mission becomes accessible from the Missions section of the Load menu. Clicking any of the missions or cutscenes listed in this area starts the game from the beginning of the selected scene/mission.

Tip

You can gain access to all missions and cutscenes without playing through the entire game. Play through the first Avalon mission. When the mission is complete, exit the game and open the *System* folder in the directory where you installed *Unreal II*. Use Notepad (or any text editing program) to open the User.ini file. Near the bottom of the file, find the AutoSaveIndex= attribute and change the value to 24 (AutoSaveIndex=24). Save the file, and restart the game. You now can access all of the missions and cutscenes from the Missions section of the Load menu.

Shields and Health

The only barriers between you and death in the field are the protective shields your battle armor generates and your health. As you absorb damage, your shields and health deplete. When your health reaches zero, you die.

Most attacks and hazards—bullets, rockets, plasma bolts, falls from high places, and so on—damage you once per "hit." Other hazards cause ongoing damage. For example, exposure to fire sets you on fire briefly and you take damage until the fire burns out. Similarly, immersing yourself in poisonous or otherwise hazardous liquid damages you continuously until you free yourself from the offending fluid.

Your health and shields automatically regenerate at the start of each new mission. In the field, however, damage accumulates every time you take a hit. Luckily, there are ways to recharge shields and health scattered throughout most levels.

The best finds are energy stations and health stations (see figure 2-8). Stepping onto these platforms recharges your shields and health (respectively). The longer you remain on the platform, the more energy or health you absorb. Energy stations are blue and health stations are orange.

Fig. 2-8. Energy and health stations.

Health and energy stations are not as common as health and energy pick-ups (see figure 2-9). These pick-ups provide a smaller boost, but they're easy to find in most areas. Simply run over them to enjoy their beneficial effects. The pick-ups follow the same color scheme as the stations—blue for energy, orange for health.

Fig. 2-9. Energy and health pick-ups.

Chapter 3: Weapons and Equipment

The weapons and equipment you carry into missions (and collect during missions) are the only things between you and annihilation at the hands of your enemies. The amount of equipment you can carry isn't an issue—the technology of the future allows you to carry a loadout rivaling that of an entire platoon. The trick is learning how to use your weapons and equipment to their maximum advantage.

This chapter gives you a rundown of the weapons and ancillary equipment you use throughout the game.

Note

Not every weapon and equipment item is available in every mission. Before you dive into the action at the start of each mission, browse through your arsenal so you don't experience any nasty surprises when you try to switch to a weapon or item that's unavailable. Even if you don't have a certain weapon at the start of a mission, one may be waiting for you to pick it up somewhere on the battlefield. Look for weapon stashes.

Weapons

Your firepower depends on the weapons you carry. Most weapons are at least marginally effective in most combat situations and against most enemies, but know the strengths and weaknesses of each offensive item at your disposal.

While your weapon-carrying capability borders on amazing, ammunition is limited—sometimes rare! To avoid wasting ammunition, understand the capabilities and limitations of your weapons.

Combat Assault Rifle

The Combat Assault Rifle (CAR) is a fully automatic weapon that fires depleted uranium shells at a high rate. The alt-fire mode fires a cluster of five shells in a single, slower-moving blast. These alt-fire clusters break up and ricochet when they hit a wall or other solid object, so you have a chance of inflicting damage from the ricochet if your shot hits near your target.

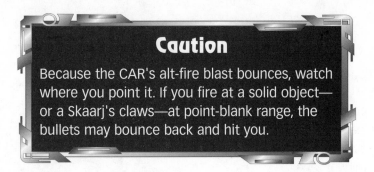

Caution

Because the CAR's alt-fire blast bounces, watch where you point it. If you fire at a solid object—or a Skaarj's claws—at point-blank range, the bullets may bounce back and hit you.

The CAR hurts light and medium enemies, and ammunition is easy to find on most levels. Don't use the CAR against heavily armored or extremely large targets if you have a more powerful alternative.

Dispersion Pistol

The T-13 Dispersion Pistol is your most basic weapon. You always have it, and it's always ready to fire because it doesn't need ammo—it recharges automatically. Its blast inflicts minimal damage and moves too slowly to hit a fast-moving target.

The Dispersion Pistol's alt-fire mode fires a more powerful blast. The amount of damage delivered depends on how long you hold down the alt-fire button. The longer you let it charge, the more powerful the blast. Your crosshairs turn red when the blast is at full strength.

Use the Dispersion Pistol as a fallback weapon for times when ammo is scarce or you're facing weak, slow-moving enemies such as local wildlife: the Snipes on Na-Koja Abad, for example.

Flamethrower

UA69 "VULCAN" FLAMETHROWER

This weapon works like you'd expect. The primary fire mode sprays out a stream of flaming napalm that sticks to your target and inflicts damage for a few seconds after the initial blast. Holding down the fire button emits a continuous flame until the ammo is depleted.

The Flamethrower's alt-fire mode sprays un-ignited napalm into the target area. The napalm sticks to most surfaces, and you can ignite the napalm by shooting it with just about any weapon (though a primary fire blast from the Flamethrower itself works best). This is a great way to set traps when you're being pursued by enemies. Wait until your target is in the napalm puddle, shoot the puddle, and watch the fun.

The Flamethrower works well against most light and medium enemies, but is somewhat ineffective against nonbiological targets (the Drakk for instance).

Caution

Don't use the Flamethrower in close quarters. If you get caught in the blast, you'll set yourself on fire. The consequences are bad if you set your enemy on fire and the creature comes into contact with you while it's still burning. The only thing worse than having a Medium Araknid jump on you is having a *flaming* Medium Araknid jump on you.

Grenade Launcher

M406 "HYDRA" GRENADE LAUNCHER

The Grenade Launcher is a versatile grenade delivery system. Pressing the fire button lobs a grenade in the direction you're aiming. The higher you aim, the greater the arc and the greater the range. Normally the grenades (regardless of type) explode on impact. However, if you hold the trigger down before you release it, a timing mechanism is engaged and the grenade bounces a couple of times before it explodes. A direct hit scores the most damage on your target, but a near miss causes proximity damage.

Six grenade types are available (though seldom all in the same mission):

- **Fragmentation Grenade:** This high explosive charge releases needle-sharp fragments when it detonates. This is the most common grenade type available.

- **Incendiary Grenade:** This explosive charge sprays burning phosphorous throughout its blast radius, briefly setting almost anything in the target area on fire.

- **EMP Grenade:** The electromagnetic pulse this releases permanently disables most small electronic devices. This grenade shuts down Plasma Field Generators with a single shot and is also effective against Auto Turrets. Larger systems aren't usually affected.

- **Concussion Grenade:** The blast this produces knocks most targets to the ground for a few moments.

- **Smoke Grenade:** This grenade releases a thick cloud of smoke concealing you from your enemies while you take cover or run away.

- **Toxic Grenade:** A slowly spreading cloud of lethal gas releases on impact. Deadly against light targets and effective against other biological threats, Toxic Grenades have limited effect against mechanical targets.

Alt-fire switches between grenade types when you have multiple varieties available.

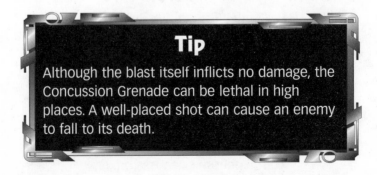

Tip

Although the blast itself inflicts no damage, the Concussion Grenade can be lethal in high places. A well-placed shot can cause an enemy to fall to its death.

Aiming grenades takes practice, and hitting targets is difficult at first. But, when you've mastered the skill, this weapon is arguably better than the Rocket Launcher due to the variety of ammunition types available.

Laser Rifle (Drakk)

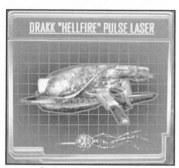

DRAKK "HELLFIRE" PULSE LASER

Isaak puts together the Drakk Laser Rifle after the Na-Koja Abad mission. A medium-range weapon, the rifle's primary fire is a railgun-like laser blast.

The Drakk Laser Rifle's alt-fire mode is a short-range sustained laser beam that fires continuously as you hold down the alt-fire button. In addition to inflicting a great deal of damage—the longer you hold the beam on your target, the more damage you inflict—the beam sets targets aflame.

This is the optimum weapon against Drakk, but it works well on most other targets too.

Note

The alt-fire mode for the Drakk Laser Rifle is available in the last two missions of the game—Avalon and *Dorian Gray*.

Pistol (Magnum)

P400 "AVENGER"

After the Hell mission, Aida gives you her magnum, "Grace," as a backup weapon. This powerful pistol fires 50-caliber rounds in primary fire mode, and alt-fire mode releases a three-round burst. The rate of fire is moderate at best in primary mode, and considerably slower in alt-fire. The Pistol shines at medium range, where it inflicts damage comparable to the Shotgun with accuracy that approaches that of the Sniper Rifle.

Despite the fact that the Pistol works well against most light and medium human-sized targets, the practicality of the weapon is limited due to the scarcity of ammunition in most missions. Use the Pistol only as a backup when your other weapons are low on ammo.

Rocket Launcher

With the Rocket Launcher, what you see is what you get. In primary fire mode, it launches a cluster of powerful, high explosive rockets at your target. A direct hit inflicts massive injury, and the collateral damage from a near miss isn't too shabby either.

The alt-fire mode lets you select up to four separate targets and launch guided rockets at each. Hold down alt-fire and hold your crosshairs on each target until you hear a beep. When all targets are selected, release the alt-fire to launch the attack. Any of the four rockets that are not assigned targets follow a winding course in the general direction you're aiming. Alt-fire takes a lot of practice. It also takes time to target the rockets, meaning you must be in a safe position and your targets must be in sight until you finish selecting them.

Needless to say, the Rocket Launcher is effective against targets of all shapes and sizes. Its only drawback is the low velocity of the rockets. If a target sees them coming, it can usually get out of the way. Use this weapon only at medium and long range unless you want to take damage.

Shock Lance (Energy Rifle)

The Izarians you encounter in the early missions carry Shock Lances. Isaak has modified yours to give it a little more kick. The primary fire emits two plasma bolts with each shot. These blasts aren't powerful individually, but the Shock Lance's high rate of fire lets you deliver a lot of hits on a target in rapid succession. The plasma bursts bounce off some surfaces (depending on the angle at which they hit), so watch out for ricochets.

The Shock Lance's alt-fire mode emits an electromagnetic pulse similar to the one produced by the EMP Grenade, but slightly less powerful.

Shock Lances are useful only against lightly armored enemies. Use this weapon as a backup when your Shotgun and CAR ammo run low. The EMP effects of the alt-fire mode are quite useful when you run out of EMP Grenades or when they're unavailable.

Shotgun

The Shotgun is a semiautomatic weapon that works just like its present-day counterparts. The primary fire is a 12-gauge blast that is extremely effective at close range. At medium range, the damage potential is greatly reduced, and long-range combat with this weapon is impossible.

The alt-fire delivers a short-range spread of incendiary pellets that ignite on impact. The result is similar to that of the Incendiary Grenade—a flaming, thrashing victim—but the damage inflicted is considerably less.

The Shotgun is a good weapon for close-quarters fighting. It is more effective on a shot-for-shot basis than the CAR, and ammunition is usually plentiful.

Singularity Cannon

This powerful weapon is available in the game's last mission—*Dorian Gray* (see Chapter 18). You don't just find Singularity Cannons lying around the ship, though. They're attached to the arms of Toscs, and are the creatures' primary mode of attack until you hurt them enough to make them drop the weapon.

The Singularity Cannon fires a burst of energy that forms an unstable micro-black hole that remains in place for a few seconds. The black hole draws any matter (or creatures) within its radius into the singularity, inflicting a great deal of damage (and, in many cases, destroying the object or creature).

This is the ideal weapon to use against the Tosc.

Sniper Rifle

The Sniper Rifle is the best long-range weapon available. It fires a 50-caliber round with pinpoint accuracy from as far as two kilometers away. You can take out most light and medium enemies with a single shot. Heavier bad guys require two or more shots, although a single shot to the head sometimes does the trick.

Alt-fire controls the sniper scope, and the Mousewheel zooms in and out. The scope is ostensibly for shooting, but also provides a means for scouting out a target area from long-range. You don't have binoculars, so the scope is the next best thing.

The Sniper Rifle has two drawbacks—scarce ammunition and slow rate of fire. Use the weapon for its designated purpose—taking out targets at long range. Not only is the Sniper Rifle impractical at close range, but it can also get you killed if you're fighting multiple targets. The amount of time that elapses between Sniper Rifle shots allows your enemy to inflict a lot of damage on you from medium- or short-range between rounds if the first shot doesn't kill them.

SpiderGun

Isaak puts together the SpiderGun using the Araknid biomass you encounter during the Hell mission. In primary fire mode, the gun fires a pod that breaks if it hits a living target, releasing a swarm of Light Araknids that attack the target. (If the pod misses the target, the pod is destroyed.) The alt-fire option has two modes. Tapping the alt-fire releases a pod trap that bursts and releases a swarm of Light Araknids when an enemy steps into its detection range. Holding down the alt-fire briefly and releasing it creates a pod that releases a Medium Araknid that attacks your enemy. The Araknids created by the Spidergun are harmless to you but deadly to your enemies.

This weapon works better as a distraction than as a practical piece of offensive ordnance. The Araknids unleashed don't do enough damage to kill most targets in a single shot, but they keep your enemy busy for a few seconds.

Takkra

Takkras are automated smart weapons that serve both offensive and defensive roles. The primary fire mode launches the Takkra at an acquired target. The weapon circles around the target and pelts it with energy blasts until the Takkra (or the target) is destroyed.

Alt-fire sets the Takkra for defensive rather than offensive operation. In this mode, the weapon follows you and attempts to shoot down all incoming projectiles. It's not 100 percent effective, but it reduces damage in situations where the enemy uses heavy projectile weapons such as Rocket Launchers.

Takkras are rare and available late in the game. Once you launch them you can't get them back, so don't waste them on small targets. Hoard them and launch them only in situations where you must deal with heavy enemies and/or boss creatures.

Equipment

You never leave the *Atlantis* with anything more than a basic loadout of

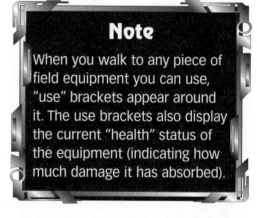

Note

When you walk to any piece of field equipment you can use, "use" brackets appear around it. The use brackets also display the current "health" status of the equipment (indicating how much damage it has absorbed).

the weapons, but several missions provide you additional equipment to aid your efforts. You must know how this equipment works and what each item is capable of in order to properly use it.

Auto Turret

The Auto Turret is a pair of machine guns mounted on a tripod equipped with sensors and an automatic firing mechanism that discriminates between friendly and unfriendly targets. When an enemy enters the detection range of the turret, the guns orient on the target and open fire. Auto Turrets have an unlimited ammo supply, and they continue to perform their function until they are destroyed. They are effective at short and medium range.

In missions where you access one or more Auto Turrets, pick them up by stepping up to them and pressing the Use control. To deploy an Auto Turret, select it from your inventory and press the primary fire control. The turret deploys in the direction you face. The direction the turret faces is important, because the device's detection and firing arc is limited (45 degrees in the direction it faces). You can pick up and move Auto Turrets whenever you want during the mission. When they're in your inventory, you carry them around with your other weapons and equipment.

In many missions, you encounter enemy Auto Turrets. Approach them from the side or from behind if possible, where you are out of their detection arc. Any weapon can inflict enough damage to destroy Auto Turrets, but stick to weapons that pack a punch and have a range greater than the turret's. That way, you can handle the Auto Turrets before they fire on you.

Tip

A direct hit from an EMP Grenade usually destroys an enemy Auto Turret.

Plasma Field Generator

Plasma Field Generators let you set up forcefields to block narrow access points. They are useful in defensive missions. In fact, when you need them most, Plasma Field Generators are always provided.

The generators work in pairs or groups. Any two generators deployed within range of one another (about four body-widths or so) automatically generate a forcefield between them that's impenetrable to weapons and solid objects. (If more than one generator is within range, forcefields are generated between all of the generators.)

You can pick up and move Plasma Field Generators like Auto Turrets (see "Auto Turrets" earlier in this chapter for details). You can also temporarily allow passage through the field by stepping up to it and pressing the Use control. A pair of Plasma Field Generators continues to generate the forcefield between them until one is destroyed.

You encounter enemy Plasma Field Generators several missions before you get a chance to play with them. You can destroy enemy generators with any weapon, but the higher the damage potential, the better. Weapons that generate an electromagnetic pulse—the EMP Grenade or the alt-fire mode of the Shock Lance—are your best choices for quickly knocking out Plasma Field Generators.

Caution

In missions where you've deployed Plasma Field Generators, avoid firing into or near the forcefield. Your weapons damage the Plasma Field Generators like enemy attacks. Don't help the bad guys get through your own forcefield!

Rocket Turret

Rocket Turrets are the big brothers of Auto Turrets. Instead of machine guns, these weapons are essentially automated Rocket Launchers. With an unlimited supply of rockets, they're devastating at any range.

In terms of deployment and field of fire, Rocket Turrets are identical to Auto Turrets, although their other operational specifications differ. Their greater attack range over Auto Turrets is coupled with a greater target detection range, which makes a close approach more difficult. The best bet for destroying an enemy Rocket Turret is to fight fire with fire—use your Rocket Launcher and attack from long-range.

Chapter 4: Allies and Enemies

In every *Unreal II* mission, you interact with a number of characters and creatures. Most (but not all) of these interactions consist of setting your sights on the other being and pulling the trigger.

Become acquainted with the cast of characters before you wade into the action. In the case of your enemies, know their abilities, strengths, and weaknesses so that you can deal with them properly. For some of your allies—specifically, the marines who follow you into battle in some missions—you need the same information so that you know what to expect of them when they fight at your side. In the case of your other allies, the members of your crew, for instance…well, it's just nice to know something about the people you're working with.

This chapter gives you all of the information you need about all of the beings you encounter in the game.

Allies

You have quite an impressive assortment of allies in *Unreal II*. Most of them are present for moral support and mission briefings or, in some cases, to open doors and access systems in secure installations. Others are there to fight at your side when the going gets tough in certain missions.

Your Crew

The friendly characters you interact with most are the crew of your starship, the *Atlantis*. These three officers provide you with mission and weapon briefings before most missions, and keep the ship up and running while you're planetside blasting bad guys. They also reveal much of the game's background story.

Two of these officers—Aida and Isaak—are ex-marines like you. The other officer, Ne'Ban, was recently assigned to the *Atlantis* as your pilot.

Aida

Aida, your first officer, was a child prodigy and a 3D chess champion at an early age. Her analytical mind made her an ideal addition to the marines, and she was drafted. She was involved in the Strider Wars, a conflict that took place a decade ago. In that war, she was forced to make a decision that caused the deaths of hundreds of innocent people. Although her brilliant military move ultimately saved *millions* of lives, she resigned her commission afterward, unable to live with the memory.

Aida doesn't entirely trust anyone—especially military authorities. She is particularly critical of Isaak because of another military incident in which both of them served.

As your first officer, Aida conducts most of your mission briefings. She also provides you with in-mission support via your communications link, and remotely hacks into security and other systems to help clear your path in hostile situations.

Isaak

Your engineer and weapons officer, Isaak, is an ex-marine like you and Aida. His military career ended after he froze in a critical situation. It was this incident that caused Aida to judge him so harshly. It also caused Isaak to hit the booze—a habit he gave up to serve with you aboard the *Atlantis*.

Isaak is a weapons expert and is usually available after your mission briefings to provide you with descriptions of your weapons and ammunition. From time to time, he even makes special modifications to existing weapons or cobbles together entirely new weapons from scratch.

Ne'Ban

Ne'Ban, the newest member of your crew, is an extremely accomplished Hex-Core pilot. The TCA assigned him to the *Atlantis* because Ne'Ban is an important being on his planet, and your patrol is supposedly the safest around.

As your pilot, Ne'Ban is responsible for ferrying you back and forth from the *Atlantis* to your various mission sites. His role is less active than those of Aida and Isaak, but his presence on the ship—and his insatiable curiosity—reveal many interesting background facts about the other members of the crew and the game situation in general. It's usually worth listening to what he has to say, but almost never mandatory to do so.

The Marines

On several missions, you work side-by-side with marine officers. In some missions, such as the Swamp mission (see Chapter 8), they simply fight alongside you. In others, you're in command and they do your bidding. Either way, the marines are there to provide you with extra firepower—and, perhaps more importantly, to provide extra targets for your enemies to shoot at—when you need them.

Fig. 4-1. From left to right: Light, Medium, and Heavy Marines.

There are three different marine types in the game, each of which has his own characteristics and appearance (see figure 4-1).

- **Light Marines** wear minimal armor and tend to carry light weaponry or Sniper Rifles. They are extremely mobile, and are a good match for similarly equipped mercenaries in a one-on-one fight. They thrive on medium- and long-range combat, but cannot last long on the front lines.

- **Medium Marines** are better protected and tend to survive longer in firefights than their Light counterparts, but they pay for their added protection with slightly impaired mobility. Armament is varied, but tends to be heavier than that carried by Light Marines.

- **Heavy Marines** are the backbone of any marine contingent. Their thick armor and powerful default weaponry allow them to stand fast against heavily armed enemies, even when outnumbered. They move slowly, but they are excellent at defending stationary locations for extended periods of time.

Other Allies

Fig. 4-2. Your other allies (from left to right): Commander Hawkins, Raff, Jensen, and Dr. Meyer.

During your travels, you meet a number of allies who either stick with you throughout the game or provide you with help or information when you need it in a specific location (see figure 4-2). Your allies include:

- **Commander Hawkins:** Your TCA sector commander

- **Raff:** The TCA drill instructor who guides you through the Avalon training course (see Chapter 5)

- **Jensen:** A lab technician who helps you through some of the security doors in the Hell mission (see Chapter 9)

- **Dr. Meyer:** A scientist who helps you escape the complex on Janus (see Chapter 14)

Enemies

During your tour of duty as a TCA marshal, you spend most of your time in the field dealing with all sorts of enemies—alien and otherwise. Before you dive headlong into the fray, know what you're facing. The following sections give you the lowdown on the creatures and mercenaries that are actively out to kill you in *Unreal II*.

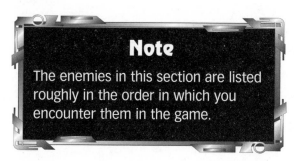

Note

The enemies in this section are listed roughly in the order in which you encounter them in the game.

Table 4-1 shows which enemies are present on each level. Many enemies have multiple classes—light, medium, heavy, and so on. Expect a mix of all classes on levels where these enemies are present.

Table 4-1. Enemies Present on Each Game Level

Mission	Izarians	Skaarj	Araknids	Izanagi Mercs	Liandri Mercs	Drakk	Tosc
Sanctuary	X	X	—	—	—	—	—
Swamp	X	X	—	—	—	—	—
Hell	—	—	X	—	—	—	—
Acheron	—	—	—	X	—	—	—
Severnaya	—	—	—	X	—	—	—
Kalydon	—	—	—	—	X	—	—
Sulferon	—	—	—	X	—	—	—
Janus	—	—	—	X	X	—	—
Na-Koja Abad	—	—	—	X	—	X	—
NC962VIII	—	—	—	—	—	X	—
Avalon	—	X	—	—	—	—	—
Dorian Gray	—	—	—	—	—	—	X

Izarians

The Izarians are a psychotic race of aliens who once ruled a small area of space, subjugating the species therein. They weren't prepared for the arrival of the Skaarj, however, and were quickly subjugated themselves. The Izarians now work exclusively as foot soldiers for their much stronger conquerors.

The Izarians' primary mode of attack is the Shock Lance (see Chapter 3 for details), although their weapons are less powerful than the version that is available to you in later missions. If they get close, they stop firing and use their weapons to jab and poke you into submission.

More of a nuisance than a real threat, Izarians are easily dispatched unless they attack in great numbers. They sometimes ambush you by jumping out from behind something, but they seldom use cover in combat. Their main strength is their movement—they move quickly and erratically, making it difficult to target them at range.

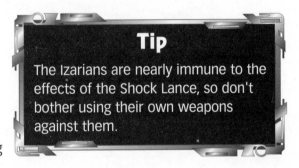

Tip

The Izarians are nearly immune to the effects of the Shock Lance, so don't bother using their own weapons against them.

Skaarj

The Skaarj are the only creatures from the first *Unreal* game who make an appearance in *Unreal II*. This race of dangerous warriors has a clan-based society, and in the past the clans seldom cooperated with one another. Lately, however, the Skaarj clans have started working together with the common goal of collecting the same seven alien artifacts that you seek.

The Skaarj don't carry weapons per se (unless you count their claws), but they launch a variety of attacks. There are three Skaarj classes—Light, Medium, and Heavy. The type and severity of their attacks varies by class.

Light Skaarj

Light Skaarj are the weakest of their kind but, even so, they do quite a bit of damage. They launch low-powered energy blasts at range, but they prefer to use their claws. When they see you, they approach with surprising speed for such large creatures.

Light Skaarj are very agile, and can leap, spin, and dodge, inflicting lots of damage with their claws, and making it difficult to draw a bead on them. To make matters worse, they block many attacks using their claws, so lighter weapons—the CAR and the Shock Lance for instance—have a limited effect (although a single, lucky alt-fire blast from the CAR can take out a Light Skaarj).

Tip

Your best bet for dealing with *any* Skaarj is to take it out at long range. Their speed and leaping ability make it difficult to escape them when they move into close range.

Medium Skaarj

Medium Skaarj are sheathed in armor, so you must inflict more damage to kill them—that's the bad news. The good news is that they aren't as agile as the Light variety, so Medium Skaarj are easier to hit. They're still very fast, however, so keep them at a distance if possible.

Medium Skaarj attack strategies differ little from Light Skaarj. They close in immediately, lobbing energy bolts (stronger than those hurled by Light Skaarj) as they approach. Once at point-blank range, they attack with their claws. They aren't as acrobatic as their unarmored compatriots, but they are just as tenacious.

Heavy Skaarj

Heavy Skaarj generally appear only as "boss" creatures at the end of levels—and it's a good thing! These heavily armored behemoths are tough to kill.

The Heavy Skaarj attack pattern differs from that of the other Skaarj. Encumbered by their armor, they lack the grace and agility needed for subtle hand-to-hand combat. Their preferred attack method is launching energy blasts from medium range. They have two types at their disposal—a yellow-white blast similar to (but about three times stronger than) that of a Light Skaarj, and a super-powerful red energy ball that inflicts massive damage. If, by chance, the Skaarj *does* get to point-blank range, a single claw attack knocks you back about 20 feet—at which point the creature starts blasting you again.

Tip

You can avoid the Heavy Skaarj's red energy blast if you are observant and time your movements. Before the Skaarj fires the blast, it bends over and folds its arms. When you observe this behavior, run and hide behind something. Wait until the energy blast explodes before you advance on the creature.

At long range, defeat a Heavy Skaarj by keeping your distance, moving constantly, and pounding the creature with your heaviest weapon. (A good time to unleash a shot on the Skaarj is when it's winding up to fire its red energy blast.) At close range, use all possible cover. Keep your head down when the red energy blasts are flying and attack between the Skaarj's shots. These guys eventually go down, but you're likely to sustain damage before they do.

Araknids

Araknids are a heretofore-unknown eight-legged alien race that resembles the Terran spider in general shape, if not in size. You encounter these creatures on Hell, but they aren't indigenous to that world. They are lab creatures that were brought to the facility and subjected to experiments that led to amazing—and extremely dangerous—mutations.

The Hell experiments produced three varieties of Araknid—Light, Medium, and Heavy.

Light Araknid

Light Araknids aren't very dangerous individually. Unfortunately, they seldom attack that way. The power of these relatively small creatures is in numbers. They have no ranged attack—their only offensive mechanism is their bite. When a swarm of Light Araknids spots you, they're on top of you in a matter of seconds.

Deal with these pesky creatures with an area effect weapon. The Flamethrower is best, but the Shotgun is also good in a pinch. If you can catch them at a distance, explosives also work well.

Light Araknids hatch out of pods scattered around the deeper sections of the Hell level. If you get close to a pod, it breaks open and unleashes its inhabitant (see figure 4-3). When you see a pod, destroy it from a distance so you don't have to deal with the Araknid within.

Fig. 4-3. A Light Araknid hatches and attacks if you get too close to a pod.

Caution

The most insidious thing about Light Araknids is their ability to move in under your line of sight and bite your ankles while you're concentrating on something else. In the Hell mission, make it a habit to look down at the floor every so often during the heat of battle to make sure no Light Araknids have gotten close without your being aware of it.

Medium Araknid

Medium Araknids are more formidable than their Light counterparts. They have no ranged attack, but they can jump great distances. They often attack in conjunction with Light Araknids—the smaller creatures augment the Medium Araknid's attack by gnawing on your legs while you concentrate your fire on the larger creature.

Whereas the best weapon to use against Light Araknids is the Flamethrower, it is *not* a good idea to use this weapon on Medium Araknids. If the initial blast doesn't kill the creature, you'll have a giant flaming spider leaping onto your head. Use the CAR or the Shotgun instead.

Heavy Araknid

It isn't until the end of the Hell mission that you see the full potential of the Araknid species. This creature is nowhere near as fast as a Light Araknid and nowhere near as nimble as the Medium variety. It doesn't have to be. In addition to its physical attack (which is extremely powerful), the Heavy Araknid has two ranged attacks. The first is a blast of web-like material that the creature flings from medium range. The webs don't entangle you, but they do cause damage. The more webs that hit you, the greater the damage. Luckily, the webs travel slowly enough that, given enough room, you can dodge most of them.

The second attack is, potentially, a lot deadlier. The Heavy Araknid generates pods. These pods (the same as the ones you encounter elsewhere on the Hell level) hatch into Light Araknids. The Light Araknids, in turn, enter the beam in the center of the room where your encounter with the giant creature takes place and become Medium Araknids. Within seconds of launching its pods, the Heavy Araknid has a small army to back it up.

For advice on surviving the Heavy Araknid encounter, see Chapter 9.

Izanagi Mercenaries (Ghost Warriors)

The mercenaries who work as enforcers for the Izanagi Corporation are a tough, resourceful group of thugs. Known as the "Ghost Warriors," some of these soldiers follow the Samurai code of ancient Japan. That doesn't really show in their combat style, however—you won't see any of them wielding katanas. They are skilled, well-trained modern day warriors who attack with any ranged weapon at their disposal.

Izanagi Mercs have three different armor configurations, each tougher than the next (see figure 4-4). The armor style defines the behavior and abilities of the merc.

Fig. 4-4. From left to right: Light, Medium, and Heavy Izanagi Mercs.

- **Light Izanagi** take relatively little damage to kill. They are, however, the fastest of the three and tend to retreat to cover when available rather than fight in the open.

- **Medium Izanagi** are harder to kill than their lighter counterparts, though their behavior pattern is similar. They are slower-moving (and, thus, easier to hit), but they tend to carry heavier weapons.

- **Heavy Izanagi** are slow and lumbering, but they can afford to be. Their heavy armor provides excellent protection—they can absorb quite a few hits, even from the Sniper Rifle. They are usually armed with heavy, long-range weapons as well. Heavy Izanagi are easily the greatest Ghost Warrior threat.

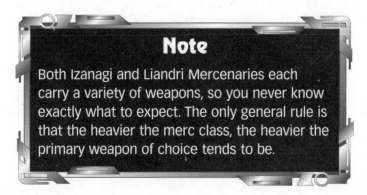

Note

Both Izanagi and Liandri Mercenaries each carry a variety of weapons, so you never know exactly what to expect. The only general rule is that the heavier the merc class, the heavier the primary weapon of choice tends to be.

Liandri "Angel" Mercenaries

The Angels are a group of elite industrial mercenaries employed exclusively by the Liandri Corporation. Genetically engineered, the Angel Mercs are trained as warriors from an early age, and are among the most skilled human fighters you encounter.

Note

Unlike the Izanagi Mercs, the Liandri Angels often work as a group during a massed attack—some lay down covering fire and keep you busy while others stealthily flank your position. This is most obvious in the Kalydon mission. (See Chapter 12 for details.)

Like the Izanagi, Liandri Mercenaries come in three varieties (see figure 4-5).

Fig. 4-5. From left to right: Light, Medium, and Heavy Liandri Angel Mercs.

- **Light Angels** are lightly armored and relatively easy to kill—if you can hit them. They are faster and more nimble than their Izanagi counterparts, so it is often hard to draw a bead on them. They take full advantage of local cover, and often manage to get past you even when you *think* you're watching them closely.

- **Medium Angels** have heavier armor and tend to carry longer-range weapons than the Light variety. The weight of the armor doesn't slow them down as much as does the medium armor worn by the Izanagi.

- **Heavy Angels** sport not only extra armor and heavier weapons, but have the ability to fly as well. Their flying armor makes them extremely mobile and dangerous. When you spot a Heavy Angel among your Liandri opponents, always make that enemy your primary target. The sooner the Heavy Angels are out of the way, the safer you are.

Tip

Both Heavy Liandri and Heavy Izanagi can absorb several Sniper Rifle shots to the body because of their thick armor, but a single, clean shot to the head is usually all it takes to put one down.

The Drakk

The Drakk are a race of self-replicating, self-repairing, sentient machines that killed their organic creators centuries ago. These flying robots are extremely tough, and low-powered terrestrial weapons tend to have a limited effect on them. The Drakk Laser Rifle and EMP weapons (EMP Grenades and the alt-fire mode of the Shock Lance) are your best offensive choices when available.

There are four Drakk classes—Light, Medium, Boss, and Droid—all of which behave quite differently from one another.

Light Drakk

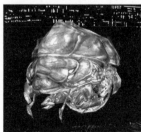

Light Drakk are fairly easy to deal with. They move at a moderate speed and have no ranged attack. They inflict damage by zapping you with an electrical charge emitted from their tentacles, which extend when they get close to you. If you destroy from long range (and leave plenty of room behind you to back away if they get close), Light Drakk aren't much of a threat.

Medium Drakk

 Medium Drakk are much more formidable than the Light variety. These creatures attack from medium range with a powerful energy blast that causes serious damage. A targeting beam guides the energy blast (which is identical to the primary fire mode of the Drakk Laser Rifle—see Chapter 3 for details). Once the beam is locked on to you, it is difficult, if not impossible, to dodge.

There are three important secrets for dealing with Medium Drakk:

- **Listen for the sound.** Medium Drakk always emit a droning sound before they appear, announcing their imminent arrival and giving you a moment to locate the source of the sound and prepare to fire.

- **Watch for the targeting beam.** Before they fire, Medium Drakk lock on to you with their targeting beam. When the beam appears, you have a second or two to blast the Drakk before it gets off a shot.

- **Don't leave them for dead.** Just because a Medium Drakk drops to the floor doesn't mean that it's dead. If there is a Drakk Droid in the vicinity, the smoking remains are repaired in a matter of seconds, putting you right back where you started (see Drakk Droid later in this chapter for details). When a Medium Drakk falls to the floor, shoot it again so there's nothing left for the Droid to repair.

Note

Injured Medium Drakk that are not repaired by Drakk Droids within about 30 seconds self-destruct on their own.

Drakk Boss

A Drakk Boss is the ultimate evolution of the species. When encountered in the open, the Drakk Boss is extremely agile. It easily dodges slow weapons, so the alt-fire EMP pulse from the Shock Lance, which works so well on other Drakk, is all but useless against the Drakk Boss. It's also difficult to score a hit with the Rocket Launcher beyond medium range.

In its initial form, the Drakk Boss attacks with an energy weapon similar to that of the Medium Drakk, but faster and twice as powerful.

Tip

There is a shorter lull between a Boss Drakk's targeting beam and the blast than there is with a Medium Drakk, but this moment of immobility is still the best time to launch a shot at the Drakk Boss. It can't dodge your shot when it's charging up for its own blast.

The Drakk can split into two creatures and, when it does, its attack changes. The top half fires a short-range continuous laser beam (identical to the alt-fire mode of the Drakk Laser Rifle—see Chapter 3 for details). The bottom half attacks with an electrical pulse similar to that of the Light Drakk, but ranged. After the creature separates, the bottom half generates a new top half. When this happens, the old top half, if it still exists, explodes after attempting an attack run.

Your only encounter with a Drakk Boss is at the end of the NC962VIII (Drakk Hive Planet) mission. See Chapter 16 for details on this encounter.

Drakk Droid

Drakk Droids are the worker bees of the Drakk homeworld. They don't pose a direct threat to you, and have no offensive weaponry whatsoever. Most of the time, they lie dormant inside their translucent chambers, but even when they're out and about, they don't hurt you.

Drakk Droids activate when an injured Medium Drakk is lying nearby. As soon as the injured Drakk is detected, the Droid scuttles out and repairs it. In a matter of seconds, the Medium Drakk is as good as new.

As long as you make sure the Medium Drakk you encounter are dead before you move on, Drakk Droids aren't an issue. If you do happen to leave an injured Medium Drakk behind and you see a Droid heading toward it, blast the Droid immediately (they're easy to kill), then finish off the Medium Drakk.

Tosc

The Tosc are giant mutant creatures that you face during the final mission aboard the *Dorian Gray* (see Chapter 18).

These behemoths are among the toughest enemies you face. They are slow moving and easy to hit, but it takes a huge amount of conventional firepower to bring them down—Rocket and Grenade Launchers are the weapons in your basic arsenal that work best.

Tosc have two ranged attack modes. The first is the deadly Singularity Cannon, which they use for medium- to long-range attacks. (The effects of the Singularity Cannon are described in Chapter 3.) Their other attack is a green energy beam that they use when they are too close for the Singularity Cannon. At point-blank range, the Tosc forgo their ranged attacks and beat you silly with their huge clawed hands.

Tip

After it takes a significant amount of damage, a Tosc drops its Singularity Cannon. Make it a point to pick up this weapon and use it against the creature (and any other Tosc you encounter). The Singularity Cannon is the best weapon available for dealing with Tosc.

When you're fighting a Tosc, keep moving and keep your distance. Despite the danger of the Tosc's Singularity Cannon attacks, you have to stay far enough away from the creature as you fight so that you don't get caught in the blast of your own high-explosive weapons. Any weapons that are safe enough to use at close range don't inflict enough damage to kill the Tosc before it kills you.

Miscellaneous Creatures

Besides your allies and active enemies, you encounter additional creatures in your travels. Some are harmless, while others—most notably the wildlife found on certain planets—can inflict injury if you don't avoid them.

Muckhog

Muckhogs are indigenous to the frozen wastes of Hell. If you follow the walkthrough outlined in Chapter 9, chances are you'll never encounter one. These creatures are usually docile if left to their own devices, but immediately attack if fired upon. Steer clear of them and save your ammo—and your health—for the enemies inside the Hell complex.

Seagoat

Seagoats are small creatures that wander the forests of Sanctuary in the Swamp mission (see Chapter 8). They are completely harmless, so there's no need to waste your ammunition on them. Watch them hop, admire their cuteness, and then move on.

Rammer

 Rammers are dinosaur-like creatures that you encounter primarily in the Swamp mission (see Chapter 8). They roam throughout the forest, especially near your landing site. If you don't bother them, they won't bother you.

> **Note**
>
> There is also a caged Rammer in one of the labs on Hell. If you set it free, it steps through the beam that created the Araknids and gets *really big*. Don't worry, though—this Rammer and all of the other giant, non-Araknid creatures in the Hell labs are harmless.

Snipe

 Snipes are the most inhospitable native life forms you encounter. They wander the wilderness of Na-Koja Abad, and actively seek you out and bite you if you stand still for too long. These nasty creatures are amphibious, so if you're in the water with no enemies in sight and you hear a splash, watch out for approaching Snipes.

While they pose no serious threat if you're careful, repeated Snipe attacks whittle your health away and leave you vulnerable to your *real* enemies.

Kai

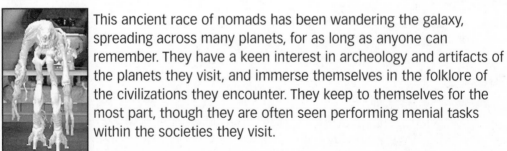 This ancient race of nomads has been wandering the galaxy, spreading across many planets, for as long as anyone can remember. They have a keen interest in archeology and artifacts of the planets they visit, and immerse themselves in the folklore of the civilizations they encounter. They keep to themselves for the most part, though they are often seen performing menial tasks within the societies they visit.

The Kai you encounter face-to-face are no threat to you—in fact, you can hardly interact with them. It isn't until the final mission of the game, *Dorian Gray*, that the Kai's role in the galaxy is revealed (see Chapter 18 for details).

Part II: Mission Walkthroughs

Now that you know how to handle yourself in the field and you have familiarized yourself with your equipment and enemies, it's time to put that knowledge to use. This tour of duty with the TCA is one of the biggest challenges of your career, and we're going to do everything we can to make things easier.

Part II of this guide provides a detailed walkthrough of every mission in *Unreal II*. Each chapter is dedicated to a different mission, and each presents you with step-by-step instructions to guide you through that mission. There are also valuable insights and advice for dealing with the hazards you will encounter along the way.

Chapter 5: Avalon (Training Mission)

Odyssey IV,
Terran Colonial Authority HQ

Your first mission is your easiest. It consists of your initial mission briefing from your commanding officer (Commander Hawkins) and the opportunity to practice your movement and combat skills on the Terran Colonial Authority (TCA) training course.

Mission Objectives:

- GO TO THE ELEVATOR.
- RUN THROUGH THE TCA TRAINING PROGRAM.
- RETURN TO YOUR SHIP.

Navigating TCA Headquarters

Legend

1. Control Room (Start)
2. Stairs to Control Room
3. Elevator

Fig. 5-1. Map of the Terran Colonial Authority Headquarters

When the mission begins, your conversation with Commander Hawkins automatically takes place. At the end of the conversation, you can run through the training course or return to your ship. Regardless of which option you select, you need to navigate to your objective.

Returning to Your Ship

Exit the control room and head down the stairs. When you reach the outdoor platform, turn right and take the stairs down as far as you can go. Turn left into the elevator and press the button to descend. Exit the elevator and head down the short staircase to end the mission.

Caution

Unlike most other levels, nothing is out to kill you in this mission. That doesn't mean you can't accidentally kill yourself! Stay away from the edges of the open platforms, and avoid jumping when you're running outside the headquarters building. It's a long way to the ground, and you can easily end your TCA career prematurely if you behave recklessly.

To the Training Course!

To proceed to the training course, exit the control room and take the stairs down to the outside platform. Turn right and take the stairs to the platform below. Follow the catwalk and turn left into the elevator. Press the button to descend to the training course.

The TCA Training Course

Legend	
1. Start	5. Firing Range
2. Control Room	6. Antechamber
3. Hologram Room	7. Combat Simulator
4. Obstacle Course	8. Energy/Health Stations

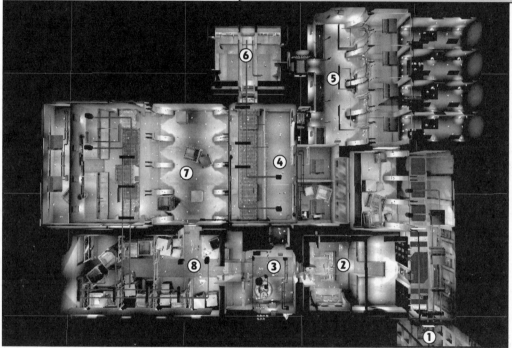

Fig. 5-2. Map of the TCA training course

Exit the elevator, turn left, and ascend the stairs to enter the training course control room. Raff, the training course technician, starts the training program. When the door to the course opens, enter.

The training course is an introduction to the game interface, equipment, and basic weapons. In the first room, Raff instructs you on the use of your heads-up display (HUD). Follow his instructions (it doesn't matter what you say to him) and proceed to the next room when he commands you to do so.

Next up is the obstacle course. Raff runs you through a few basic moves—simple jumps, mantling (jumping to a platform and pulling yourself up), and crouching.

TIP

After you perform your mantle maneuver, stay on top of the block onto which you climb. If you move forward, you drop off of the block into the shallow pit. If this happens, you have to climb up before you can perform the next task.

After you complete the obstacle course, follow Raff's instructions and enter the firing range. Here you test three weapons—the Dispersion Pistol, the Combat Assault Rifle (CAR), and the Grenade Launcher.

As Raff introduces each weapon, pick it up and move into the firing range location next to the alcove from which you retrieve the weapon. Take a few pot shots at the targets that pop up, following Raff's instructions. The door in front of the targets closes when it's time to move to the next weapon.

After you finish playing with the Grenade Launcher, Raff invites you into the final section of the training course—the combat simulator—for one-on-one combat. Load up on ammunition in the firing range alcoves, and exit the firing range. Raff gives you instructions. When the door opens, grab the ammo in the antechamber, then head into the combat simulator room.

Raff's holo-image appears in a random location. Follow the sound of his movement, and blast. The first one of you to reach five kills wins the match. Run over Raff's "corpse" after a kill to pick up his ammunition. You can't be killed, but if you reach zero health, Raff scores a point.

You can play as many combat matches as you want. Take this opportunity to practice—it's the only time you can do so in a safe environment. To leave before the match is over, exit the course through the door opposite the entrance.

After you recharge your health and shields outside the course, re-enter the control room and talk with Raff. The mission automatically ends.

Chapter 6: *Atlantis* Interlude I

After visiting Terran Colonial Authority HQ, you return to your ship, the *Atlantis*, for some down time. The *Atlantis* Interlude is not a real a mission—it's more of an introductory session where you can meet your crew and explore your ship.

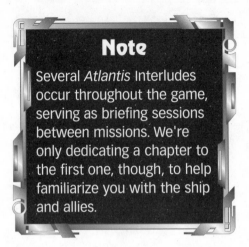

Note

Several *Atlantis* Interludes occur throughout the game, serving as briefing sessions between missions. We're only dedicating a chapter to the first one, though, to help familiarize you with the ship and allies.

Mission Objectives:

- TOUR THE *ATLANTIS* AND MEET YOUR CREW (OPTIONAL).
- LISTEN TO AIDA'S BRIEFING FOR THE SANCTUARY MISSION.
- LISTEN TO ISAAK'S WEAPONS BRIEFING (OPTIONAL).
- PROCEED TO THE DROP ROOM AND LAUNCH THE SANCTUARY MISSION.

Talking with Aida

Fig. 6-1. Your first officer, Aida.

When you come aboard, Aida greets you and gives you a status report (see figure 6-1). No matter what you say to Aida, it comes down to two choices—exploring the ship or proceeding to the briefing for the Sanctuary mission. (The Sanctuary mission is discussed in Chapter 7.)

Exploring the Atlantis

Legend	
1. Bridge	5. John's Quarters
2. Aida's Quarters	6. Isaak's Quarters
3. Briefing Room (Lower Deck)	7. Ne'Ban's Quarters
4. Armory (Lower Deck)	8. Drop Room (Lower Deck)

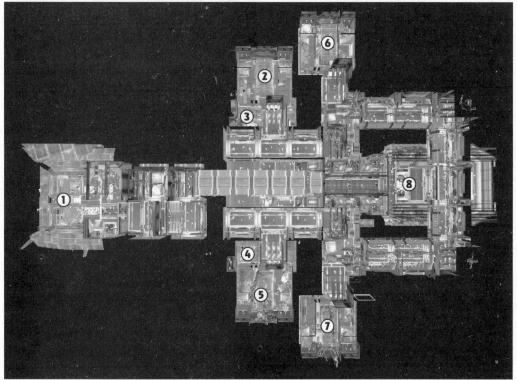

Figure 6-2. Map of the Atlantis

Explore the ship. Aida and your engineer, Isaak, show you the highlights (if you follow them). There is no time limit, so explore any or all of the ship at your leisure. Greet your new pilot, Ne'Ban. You can't interact with any of the ship's controls so, when you've taken in the sights, head to the briefing room.

The Briefing Room

If you skip the tour and head from the drop room to the briefing room, follow Aida. If you lose her, exit the drop room and follow the corridor forward. The briefing room is the first door on the right.

This huge generator provides juice for the heavy rock-crushing equipment.

Fig. 6-3. Aida gives you an overview of the Sanctuary mission.

When you enter the briefing room, interact with Aida and choose "Yes" to begin the briefing. She fills you in on the details of the upcoming Sanctuary mission (see figure 6-3).

You have to stay for the entire briefing. When it's over, Aida repeats it (interact with her for your options), or you can proceed to your weapons briefing with Isaak across the hall.

Weapons Briefing

After Aida's mission summary, exit the briefing room and proceed through the door across the

Note

You are not required to visit Isaak. If you prefer to embark immediately, proceed to the drop room after Aida's briefing.

open bay. Isaak is waiting there to give you an overview of the weapons available for the Sanctuary mission. Interact with him to start the weapons briefing.

Have him explain each of the weapons individually by selecting the appropriate option from the interaction menu. Select "No Thanks" when you're ready to end the conversation and leave. Isaak's briefing covers the same info Raff gave you in the training mission (see Chapter 5), so if you're familiar with the weapons, skip the weapons briefing and proceed to the drop room.

Ending the Interlude

After Aida's briefing, proceed to the drop room. To leave the *Atlantis* and start the Sanctuary mission, interact with the drop ship.

Chapter 7: Sanctuary

Back on the *Atlantis*, Aida informed you of the situation at the Liandri Mining Facility on Elara V (also known as Sanctuary). You are sent down on what is supposed to be a simple search and rescue mission—but the situation is more complicated than anticipated.

Mission Objectives:

- INVESTIGATE THE INSTALLATION ON SANCTUARY TO DISCOVER THE CAUSE OF THE DISTRESS CALL.
- GET TO THE GENERATOR BUILDING.
- RESCUE MILLER.
- FIND THE GENERATOR CONTROL ROOM.
- REACTIVATE THE GENERATOR.
- RETRIEVE THE ARTIFACT FROM THE BOTTOM OF THE GENERATOR.
- GET OUT OF THE GENERATOR.

Part I: Mining Complex Entrance

After the drop ship lands, head for the door across the courtyard, proceed through, and go down the stairs. Retrieve the ammo from the corpse under the staircase, then proceed through the door. At the opposite end of the corridor, an unseen attacker mauls a technician. Don't rush to his aid—you can't save him.

The door where the attacker mauls the technician doesn't open, so make a right into the service corridor. Follow the service corridor to the left and make the first right into the hallway. (An Izarian runs by—don't bother shooting at it.)

Turn right into the hallway. There's no reason to fire a weapon here, but if you do, watch for the flammable tanks scattered throughout the area. Follow the hallway to the left until you reach a large room.

Across the room, an Izarian plays with a technician's corpse. When the alien notices you, it attacks—along with a few of its friends (see figure 7-2). Dispatch the Izarians and collect their Shock Lances.

Fig. 7-2. A small army of Izarians attacks when they spot you.

Legend
1. Start
2. Underwater Area
3. Double Stairway
4. Finish

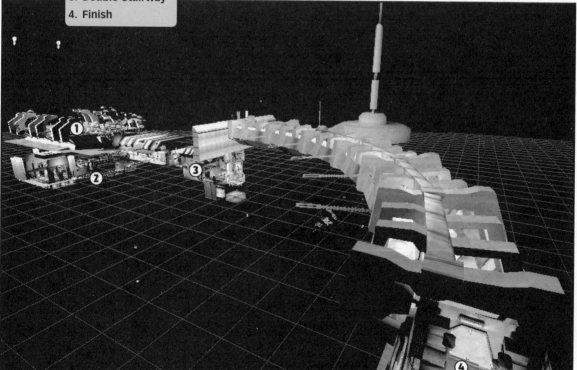

Fig. 7-1. Sanctuary map, part I

After the last Izarian is killed, a technician named Miller contacts you over the intercom system. Miller provides moral support and directs you to his location throughout the level.

When Miller opens the hatches in the floor, step through one of them and drop into the water. Explore and pick up ammo and weapons—your armor keeps you from drowning. When you're ready to move on, locate the large pipe and follow it until it parallels a second pipe. Follow both pipes until you come to the opening that leads to dry land.

When you exit the water, find the ladder and ascend. The door on this level doesn't function, so climb the stairs and go through the door at the top. Several more Izarians are on the other side. Take them out using the columns for cover, then proceed through the door at the chamber's opposite end.

Another alien is beyond the door to the right, so watch out. After it's taken care of, move forward with caution. More Izarians are on the double stairway ahead, with reinforcements in the corridor below. Hold the high ground and let the aliens come to you (see figure 7-3).

Fig. 7-3. Don't proceed down the double stairway until you've eliminated the aliens at the foot of the stairs.

Tip

Even if you think you've killed all of the Izarians on the double stairway, a few might lurk below. Stay alert!

At the bottom of the double stairway, move forward into the room beyond. (There's likely to be an additional Izarian lurking in this area.) Climb the metal ladder. When you reach the top, take out the Izarian to the right and behind you. When the area is secure, avail yourself to the weapons and health in the area and proceed through the door.

The corridor beyond is filled with boxes and explosive tanks—and Izarians are hidden among them. When you hear the aliens approaching, get into an open area away from the explosive tanks.

At first the aliens attack one at a time, but when you reach the second pile of crates, they attack en masse from all directions. Use the explosive tanks to your advantage—blast the tanks while several aliens are nearby to take out a whole group at once (see figure 7-4).

Fig. 7-4. Target the explosive tanks to take out a group of aliens in a single blast.

After you deal with the onslaught, a couple of aliens might still hang around the end of the corridor. Take them out, stock up on ammo and Shock Lances, and head through the door to proceed to the mission's next phase.

Part II: Mining Complex

When you step through the outer door, Miller tells you that there are no aliens in sight and that it's easy from here on out. Don't believe it! Izarians lurk on the rooftop of the building to your left, and leap down upon you moments after you enter the courtyard (see figure 7-6). There are more when you round the corner, both on the roof and on the ground. Retreat back around the corner if necessary to keep the Izarians from ganging up on you. Many Izarians linger near the steaming grate in the corner; blast the explosive

Fig. 7-6. Despite Miller's assurances, Izarians are lurking everywhere.

barrels to the left of the grate to take out the aliens en-masse.

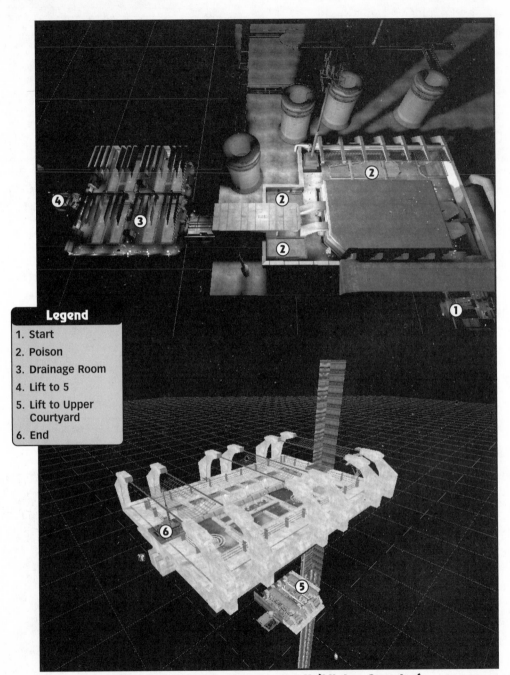

Legend
1. Start
2. Poison
3. Drainage Room
4. Lift to 5
5. Lift to Upper Courtyard
6. End

Fig. 7-5. Sanctuary map, part II (Mining Complex)

After the aliens are out of the way, proceed forward, staying clear of the green ooze to the right. Head left around the far corner; deal with the Izarians lingering there.

When the area is clear, crouch and move through the door that is opening and closing. In the corridor beyond, gather health before you proceed to the door ahead (which leads to the drainage room). As per Miller's warning, the room is full of Izarians, and they open fire when you step inside (see figure 7-7).

Fig. 7-7. Prepare for an intense firefight when you enter the drainage room.

Keep moving to avoid damage, and take out the aliens as quickly as you can.

When you reach the other side of the drainage room, Miller opens the security door for you. Grab the ammo and other goodies before you enter and activate the elevator.

After the elevator starts moving, a Skaarj jumps on the roof and sabotages the mechanism, sending you plunging down the shaft. Move to the back of the car (away from the door) and enjoy the ride—there's nothing you can do to stop it.

When you get to the bottom and the doors open, the Skaarj falls off the car. Blast it before it attacks you.

The door at the opposite end of the room is useless, so enter the lift next to the elevator (to your right as you exit), and activate it. When you reach the top of the shaft, check under the stairs for health and a shield recharge, then head up.

The door at the top of the stairs leads to an outer courtyard that's patrolled by a Skaarj (see figure 7-8). Take it out at a distance—those Skaarj claws cause serious damage. Scrounge around for ammo in the courtyard if you need it, then proceed through the door at the opposite end to move to the next part of the mission.

Fig. 7-8. Pick off the Skaarj in the garden before it gets too close.

Part III: Power Plant

Legend

1. Start (Inside)
2. Muddy Lake
3. Bridge
4. Girders
5. Reactor Control Room (Inside)
6. Reactor

Fig. 7-9. Sanctuary map, part III

Move through the door ahead and stock up on ammo before going outside. Step out and let the door close behind you—a couple of explosive tanks are inside; don't stand next to them.

When you're outside, a Skaarj attacks from the valley ahead, while Izarians lay down cover fire from the canyon rim above the door (see figure 7-10). Find cover, and take out the Skaarj, then pick off the aliens on the rim before moving forward. A few more Izarians may be on the rim above and behind you to either side, so check around before stepping into the open.

Tip

Check the muddy lake to your right as you enter the canyon for ammo and weapons.

Fig. 7-10. The Izarians firing from above make battling the Skaarj on the ground more difficult than usual.

Cross the bridge; be ready for a Skaarj ambush from the left. After you deal with the alien, proceed toward the power plant. The easiest path to the building is across the two girders that span the lake—there's no need to swim. Take the leftmost girder across, because most of the enemies you're about to face are around the corner to the right. Unfortunately, that's where you have to go.

Tip

Don't go around the left side of the building. The only thing waiting for you there is a Skaarj.

Once across, hug the building's wall and move right. When you round the far corner, a Skaarj attacks (see figure 7-11). Retreat as you fight—rushing headlong into this battle and trying to stand your ground will get you killed.

Fig. 7-11. The power plant perimeter is guarded by a Skaarj—and it doesn't want you to pass.

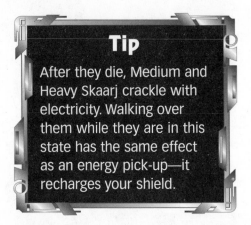

Tip

After they die, Medium and Heavy Skaarj crackle with electricity. Walking over them while they are in this state has the same effect as an energy pick-up—it recharges your shield.

When you round the corner, Miller gets cocky and runs outside to meet you, alien artifact in hand. Unfortunately, he meets his demise. You must reactivate the generator that Miller and his Skaarj attacker have fallen into and retrieve the alien artifact.

Head up the stairs and follow the catwalk around to your left. Open the emergency hatch and drop down into the room below. It's dark inside, and an Izarian waits for you below. Blast the alien, stock up on ammo, and exit the room.

Outside, follow the catwalk to the end and enter the building through the door on your left.

Moments after you arrive in the corridor upstairs, a Skaarj crashes through the window on your left. Take it out, then proceed down the corridor and through the door at the opposite end.

In the corridor beyond, you witness some Skaarj activity through the door on your right. This door doesn't open, so move down the corridor. Before you reach the red boxes, turn left and locate a hatch in the floor under the large pipe. Climb down and turn left. A Skaarj is waiting to maul you in the crawlway below.

At the opposite end of the crawlway is the room you saw through the non-working glass door above. Find an opening on your right that's big enough to move through, crouch, and enter the crawlspace under the room. Expect a Skaarj to join you from above before you reach a place where you can stand and enter the room.

There's a computer console in the room, but it's inactive. First you must activate the two emergency override switches on the wall. They're on your right as you face the door leading to the corridor (see figure 7-12). Jump across to get to them.

Fig. 7-12. Flip two switches like this one to start the reactivation sequence.

After both switches are activated, the computer console comes to life. When the computer detects the alien life-form in the generator, an override button opens on the left side of the console. Press the button to reactivate the generator.

The door to the corridor works from the inside. Exit the room, turn left, open the door, and retrace your path to the catwalk outside. Some Izarians have gathered in the corridor and in the room at the bottom of the lift, so deal with them on the way out.

You emerge on the catwalk outside. You need to get to the generator shaft's bottom. The only way is down through the mechanism itself (see figure 7-13).

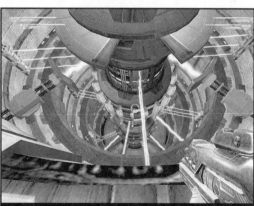
Fig. 7-13. Run this dangerous gauntlet to reach the bottom of the generator shaft.

Turn right and follow the catwalk to the door at the end. Jump over the railing to your left so that you are on the protruding point of grating that hangs over the shaft. Move out as far as you can without falling off (see figure 7-14).

Drop onto the platform that's rotating around the shaft's center. Time your drop so that you don't land in one of the openings in the platform. Stay toward the platform's outer edge so you rotate with it. If you are up against the central shaft, you can get brushed off.

Fig. 7-14. Move out as far as you can on the grating so you can drop onto the platform rotating around the center of the shaft.

Look over the edge and wait until you are positioned above one of the extending and retracting armatures. When the armature is fully extended, step off the platform and drop onto it. Before the armature collapses into the outer wall, step off and drop onto the catwalk (along the shaft's outer wall). Crouch when you land to avoid the rotating electrical discharges.

Move around the catwalk (remaining crouched) until you are over one of the next set of armatures, drop onto the armature when it is extended, then drop onto the next catwalk. Repeat this one more time (dropping to the next armature down and onto the catwalk below that). You're now on the bottom catwalk, and you can step onto the shaft's floor.

The artifact is on the ground near Miller's body. When you pick it up, a Heavy Skaarj appears and attacks (see figure 7-15). Keep moving and hit it with the most powerful weapons you've got. This is not an easy battle to win, and you're dead if you stand still.

After dispatching the Heavy Skaarj, find the elevator door in the central shaft and ride it to the top. The marines arrive and take the artifact from you when you reach the surface. Mission accomplished.

Fig. 7-15. Your final battle in the Sanctuary complex is a deadly showdown with this guy.

Chapter 8: Swamp

On the way back from the surface of Elara V, Aida informs you that the marines who retrieved the alien artifact from you were shot down in the forest on the planet's far side. It's up to you to locate the wreck and lead them to safety before whatever shot down the marine ship comes around to admire its work.

Mission Objectives:

- FOLLOW THE DIRECTIONAL BEACONS TO THE CRASH SITE.
- MAKE CONTACT WITH THE SURVIVING MARINES.
- ACCOMPANY THE MARINES TO THE CLEARING THAT HOLDS THE HOMING BEACON.
- DEFEND THE CLEARING UNTIL THE ATLANTIS ARRIVES.

Speedship Crash Site

It is dark and disorienting in the forest—it's hard to see landmarks, and it's easy to stray off course. Put your back to the drop ship. Move forward toward the swarm of fireflies, and to the left. If you run into impassible trees, follow to the left until you see the first flashing beacon.

Note

The local wildlife—Rammers and Seagoats, of which there are many around your landing site—is not dangerous, so don't waste ammo on it.

Fig. 8-2. The red beam indicates the direction of the next beacon.

The red beam emitted by each beacon points the way to the next beacon—just follow the beam (see figure 8-2). Find the first one, and you'll have no problem following the path to the crash site. If you stray off course, backtrack to the previous beacon and try again.

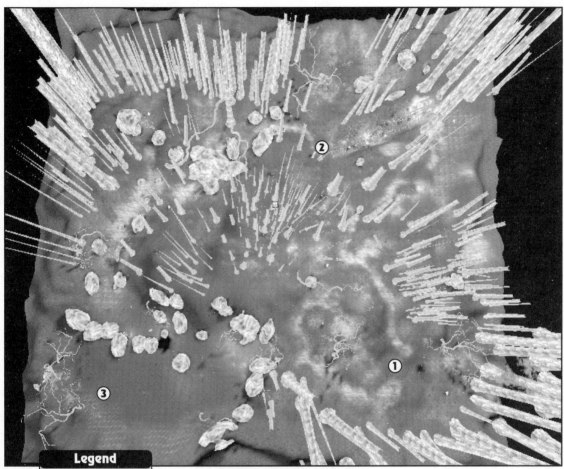

Legend
1. Start
2. Marine Crash Site
3. Finish

Fig. 8-1. Swamp map

You'll come to an area marked by burning debris and a burned-out trench. This is the start of the crash site. Follow the trail of debris until you reach the marines' perimeter (see figure 8-3).

As you approach, the marines deactivate the forcefield. After you converse with the marine leader, the marines take off in the direction of a clearing where the *Atlantis* can retrieve you. Follow the marines, and watch and listen to the commander for orders.

Fig. 8-3. Approaching the marines' perimeter forcefield.

After you leave the crash site, Izarians ambush your group (see figure 8-4). Assist the marines in eliminating the threat. Many of the aliens are hiding in and dropping from the trees above, so look in all directions. When the threat is eliminated, the marines move out. Follow them.

You run into a series of Izarian ambushes along the way. The next comes after you pass through a small cave. From that point on, one or two Izarians are around every turn in the path.

You've reached the clearing when you see ammo crates and a health station. Defend the area for five minutes while waiting for the *Atlantis* to arrive. Stock up on health and ammo after dispatching the last of the Izarians—you'll need it.

Fig. 8-4. A group of Izarians ambushes you and your marine escort after you leave the crash site.

Stay on the high ground near the beacon. The attack comes after Aida's initial communication. Follow the sound of gunfire and help the marines fend off the attack (see figure 8-5). Stick to the high ground above either perimeter forcefield—it's safer, and you have a better angle of fire.

It's a constant Izarian and Skaarj barrage from both ends of the valley for the next four minutes. Hang back and let the marines handle the lion's share of the work if you take too much of a beating. Your goal is to survive until the *Atlantis* arrives. When it does, the mission is complete.

Fig. 8-5. The aliens begin an assault four minutes before the *Atlantis* arrives.

Back on the *Atlantis*

When the *Atlantis* picks you up, you're on the bridge with Ne'Ban. After conversing with him, head to the briefing room and talk to Aida. (See figure 6-2 if you forgot the way.) She gives you the briefing for your next mission—a trip to a frozen wasteland known as Hell (see figure 8-6).

After the briefing, check in with Isaak to get a rundown of your weapons for the mission. You can skip the weapons briefing if you want, but it's worthwhile to visit Isaak. He explains two new weapons—the Shock Lance and the Shotgun.

Fig. 8-6. Visit the briefing room for the lowdown on your next mission.

When you're ready to go to Hell, go to the drop room and interact with the drop ship to start the next mission.

Chapter 9: Hell

After the Swamp mission, Aida fills you in on the situation at the Elysium Weapons Research Facility on Hell, a frozen moon. All contact has been lost, and it's your job to find out why. The situation is urgent because the researchers are examining an artifact similar to the one you recovered from Sanctuary. This won't be easy....

Mission Objectives:

- ENTER THE INSTALLATION.
- INVESTIGATE TO DETERMINE WHY CONTACT WAS LOST.
- HEAL THE SURVIVING PATIENT.
- BYPASS THE FIRE THROUGH THE SECOND STORY CONTROL ROOM.
- FIND THE CAUSE OF THE ARAKNID THREAT.
- REACTIVATE THE FAN TO VENT THE PLASMA GAS.
- GET TO THE UPPER LEVEL LAB CONTROL ROOM.

- DISENGAGE THE SECURITY LOCKDOWN.
- RETRACE YOUR PATH TO ENTER THE RESEARCH FACILITY'S CENTRAL HUB.
- GET INTO THE CENTRAL DOME.
- FIND A WAY TO BYPASS THE BARRICADE.
- DEACTIVATE THE MAIN BEAM.
- OBTAIN THE ARTIFACT.
- DEFEAT THE QUEEN.

Part I: Descent

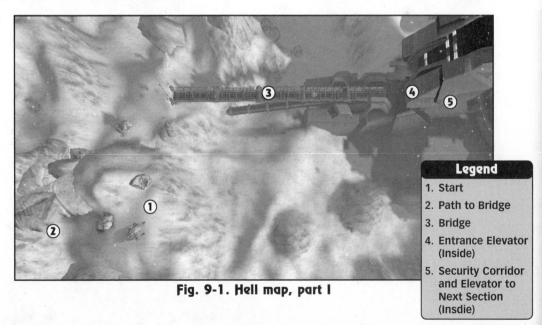

Fig. 9-1. Hell map, part I

Legend
1. Start
2. Path to Bridge
3. Bridge
4. Entrance Elevator (Inside)
5. Security Corridor and Elevator to Next Section (Insdie)

Your first task is to get from your landing site to the bridge that leads to the main facility. A straight line is out of the question—it's a long way down (see figure 9-2).

Fig. 9-2. The road to Hell is paved with snow and sheer canyon walls.

The path isn't difficult to follow. A small overhang is behind your ship to the right. Walk through the overhang, and follow the path through a narrow valley. You reach the bridge in short order. Avoid any local critters at the end of the bridge, then proceed across. The seemingly dead Muckhog on the bridge isn't dead—it's lying in wait. Kill it and proceed into the building. Step onto the round elevator and descend into Hell. Don't dawdle outside the building, or more creatures from the valley below will come up to harass you.

Note

Don't take the path to the left of the bridge, there's no point. Your goal is to cross the bridge and enter the facility. Stick to the mission profile!

When you get to the bottom of the shaft, step through the door and into the hall. When you pass the security checkpoint you are trapped by forcefields and scanned by the computer (see figure 9-3). You're in no danger. Stand still and wait. Aida shuts down the security system in time.

After the forcefields are shut down, proceed through the door at the corridor's end to enter the facility.

Fig. 9-3. Don't sweat the security checkpoint—Aida will come through.

Part II: Discovery

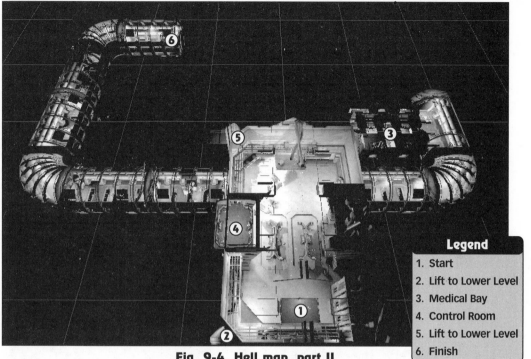

Fig. 9-4. Hell map, part II

Legend
1. Start
2. Lift to Lower Level
3. Medical Bay
4. Control Room
5. Lift to Lower Level
6. Finish

Two doors lead off of the platform you enter on, both to your left. The far door is locked and Aida can't hack the security code, so use the other door—a lift to the ops area on the lower level. After descending, cross the room and exit through the door to the right of the huge fire. Pick up the Flamethrower near the corpses on your way.

Follow the corridor. After you pass through two doors, another fire blocks your path. Enter the medical bay through the door on your left.

Patients are on the exam tables, but the one you're interested in, Jensen, is lying on the far right side. Activate the panel on the bed to heal him (see figure 9-5). He tells you that to bypass the fire in ops, you have to go through the security room on the second floor (through the locked door).

Fig. 9-5. Once healed, Jensen helps you get past the security doors. For a while, at least.

Exit the medical bay and retrace your steps to the control room with Jensen in tow. Let Jensen open the door and follow him inside. Press the button on the panel to your right to activate the audio log for an account of what went wrong at the facility. Stock up on ammo and exit through the door at the opposite end of the room. (You can pick up some additional ammo and weapons at the far end of the catwalk beyond.) When you are ready, step through the orange door and ride the lift downstairs.

Turn right and exit ops through the round door, which leads to a corridor littered with bodies. Continue through the door at the end, into the next corridor segment. When you reach the halfway point, you hear movement in the walls and Jensen panics. Back up toward the door through which you entered. In moments, the corridor is crawling with Light and Medium Araknids that drop from the vents in the ceiling (see figure 9-6). Some of them go after Jensen first, giving you a

Fig. 9-6. When you reach the halfway point in the second hallway segment, Araknids pour from the ceiling vents.

momentary respite form the onslaught. Kill all of the Araknids in the area. Be particularly careful when dealing with the Light Araknids—it's easy for them to get in under your line of sight and cause ongoing damage by biting ankles. Retreat as far as necessary to keep the Araknids in front of you.

After dealing with the Araknid onslaught, continue forward through the next two doors. When you pass the barricade of crates, the next door opens, admitting another wave of Light and Medium Araknids. Retreat behind the barricade and take them out. Additional Araknid reinforcements will arrive through the door on the other side of the barricade as you fight. When the area is clear, gather the weapons and ammo near the barricade and proceed through the door. Keep your eyes open for additional Araknids in the corridor beyond. Move through the next door when the area is secure.

As you round the curved corridor, the far door opens, admitting more Light Araknids (see figure 9-7). Deal with them and go through the door. The next corridor segment is empty. Head through the far door to begin the next part of the mission.

Fig. 9-7. These things are everywhere ....

Part III: Desolation

After the new map section loads, light Araknids wait to jump from either side of the machinery in front of you. If you stand still long enough they'll come to you. You're better off going to them—the door behind you is sealed, so your back is against the wall. Watch out for additional Light Araknids entering from the door on the right.

That door is where you're headed. It leads to the ion beam room. After you deal with the Light Araknids, go through, but hang back in the doorway. Several Medium Araknids wait for you (see figure 9-9). Deal with them before moving inside. There might be a couple Light Araknids as well if all of them didn't come out to meet you in the outer chamber, so stay alert.

Fig. 9-9. Expect an Araknid attack when you enter the ion beam room.

Legend	
1. Start (Lower Level)	6. Weapons Room
2. Ion Beam Room (Lower Level)	7. Pod-Converted Floor
3. Poison Gas Leak (Middle Level)	8. Generator
4. Entrance to Airshaft (Middle Level)	9. Ion Beam Room Catwalk (Upper Level)
5. First Pod Encounter (Middle Level)	10. Exit to Round Elevator (Finish)

Fig. 9-8. Hell map, part III (Desolation)

Check the catwalk around the ion beam for ammo, then take the lift to the upper level. The upper catwalk is crawling with Medium Araknids, so be ready. After dealing with the enemies, stock up on health and shields before moving on.

Caution

When fighting the Araknids on the upper platform in the ion beam room, don't back up too far toward the lift. The lift car is on the lower level, so backing into the lift door could cause you to tumble down the shaft.

To the left, the catwalk is blocked by a plasma gas leak, so turn right. When you get to the broken fan, crouch down and climb up into it. The airshaft above is full of Light Araknids, so be ready. A few visit you as you're climbing up—but that's just the tip of the iceberg. When you enter the upper shaft and turn right, dozens of Light Araknids come at you (see figure 9-10). Your best defense is the Flamethrower. Lay down a line of fire that fills the shaft and wipes out the aliens before they can get to you.

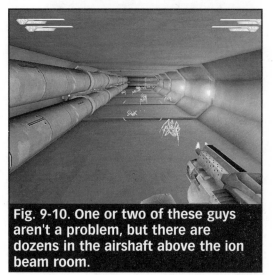

Fig. 9-10. One or two of these guys aren't a problem, but there are dozens in the airshaft above the ion beam room.

After eradicating the Light Araknid onslaught, proceed through the shaft. Round the corner, and continue to the top of a slight rise. There's another wave of Araknids awaiting you in the shaft beyond. Deal with them as you did the previous group. At the top of the rise is an observation window that overlooks the ion beam room. Use the ventilation control switch beside the window to activate a fan that clears most of the plasma gas that you saw leaking on the catwalk below. Retrace your steps through the shaft and return to the ion beam room. Follow the catwalk past the plasma gas. Stay to the far right as you move by the gas cloud to avoid damage.

When you reach the catwalk's other side, a scientist steps through the door ahead and to the left, and is killed when the pods on the wall and catwalk hatch (see figure 9-11). Remember the pods—you'll see a lot more of them. They can only hatch once, so it's safe to walk past the corpse and through the door.

Fig. 9-11. Note the protrusions on the wall on the left and the catwalk on the right. They're pods. Light Araknids burst from them if you walk too close.

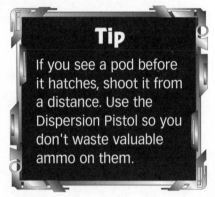

Tip

If you see a pod before it hatches, shoot it from a distance. Use the Dispersion Pistol so you don't waste valuable ammo on them.

Light and Medium Araknids are beyond the door—they might be around the corner when you enter. There's also a pod on top of the crate ahead. Deal with all of the Araknids, blast the pod, and move on down the corridor.

The first door you come to (on your left around the second turn) leads to a weapons room full of guns, ammo, health, and energy. Enter, but don't go in too far. Pods are in the room. Destroy them before you collect the booty. Check for additional pods behind the crates and shelves!

Exit the weapons room, turn left, and continue down the corridor, checking the walls for pods as you go. More Araknids are around the corner, past the pipe that's leaking fire. Stay away from the fire when you're fighting the aliens!

The door at the corridor's end leads to a catwalk above the area where you entered the Desolation section of the Hell map. When you step through, look both ways for the Araknids lying in wait. (If you pause in the doorway, rather than running through, you can blast some of them before they notice you.) Look for pods as you move around the catwalk to the door on the opposite side. Step through the door and grab the ammo and other goodies before proceeding up the ramp.

The floor upstairs is covered with pods, so clear them out with the Flamethrower (see figure 9-12) or pick them off one at a time with the Dispersion Pistol to save ammo. Light Araknids can hatch from the pods at any time (some are already lurking around), so don't stand around for too long. More pods are along the walls and past the generator. Medium Araknids also lurk in the area past the generator near the ramp. Clear the area and head up the ramp.

Fig. 9-12. The Flamethrower is great for clearing a large concentration of pods.

The catwalk upstairs is inhabited by pods and Medium Araknids. Deal with them and follow the catwalk around to the right. Retrieve the ammo by the corpse, then head through the round door.

The room beyond is crawling with Medium Araknids (see figure 9-13) and a few Light ones as well. Hang back and take out as many as you can before they come after you. You can hit several of the Medium Araknids from a distance before they attack.

When the Medium Araknids are out of the way, head around the catwalk to the right. Take out the Light Araknids and pods in the first alcove, then collect the ammo and health. Another alcove on the chamber's opposite side contains ammo and energy if you need

Fig. 9-13. Hang back and deal with the Medium Araknids near the door rather than rushing into the room.

it. Head for the exit (the round door opposite the one through which you entered). The Araknids on the other side come through the door to greet you if you wait around long enough.

Follow the corridor to the end and step through the door onto the round elevator to ascend to the next part of the mission.

Part IV: Disclosure

Legend
1. Start (Middle Level)
2. Materials Laboratory (Upper Level)
3. Central Dome Corridor (Middle Level)
4. Atmospherics Laboratory (Upper Level)
5. Biological Laboratory (Upper Level)
6. Passage from Pipe Room to Central Dome (Lower Level)
7. Artifact and Heavy Araknid (Lower Level)

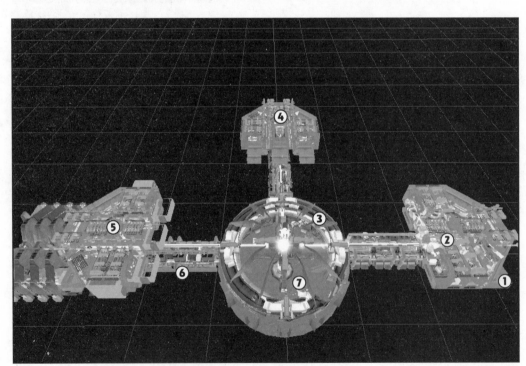

Fig. 9-14. Hell map, Part IV

The large door is locked down, and Aida informs you that you have to manually bypass it. Take the lift to the level above. The Araknids you've been fighting come from deeper in the base—and your journey from this point on won't be fun.

When you reach the materials laboratory level upstairs, you find two sealed bulkheads, one damaged bulkhead, and another lift. The top of the lift leads to the control room (your destination), but the top exit is blocked. You have to gain access the hard way.

Crouch and enter the lab through the broken bulkhead. The room is a shambles and is crisscrossed by deadly energy beams. Ammunition, health, and energy packs are scattered among the wreckage.

Fig. 9-15. The source of the energy discharges in the lab.

The lab control room is behind the window, up and to your left as you enter. Your path isn't easy. Starting at the broken bulkhead where you entered, turn left. Alternately crouch under and jump over energy beams until you reach the beam's source (see figure 9-15).

Crouch and move under the front of the generator. When you're past it, turn right and go to the room's back wall. Turn right and follow along the wall (behind the block that reflects the beam). Walk around the sloped concrete block, and jump onto the two stacked black slabs behind it.

Turn right. A series of broken pillars extends across the orange plasma-like lake. Hop from pillar to pillar until you reach the third pillar, then turn right. Step onto the stacked black slabs and turn left. A series of pillars extends from your position, angling right. Hop across them and pause when you reach the third one (the long one that is like a flat arch).

At this point, you can see the control room window, and the rest of your path is clear (see figure 9-16). Take a running leap off the end of your current perch. You don't have to make it all the way to the slated pillar—just far enough to clear the intervening energy beams and reach the pillar's base. Walk up the slanted pillar into the control room.

Fig. 9-16. The final few steps to the control room.

Inside the control room, locate the bulkhead lockdown override and plasma beam control buttons and activate them. Step onto the slanted pillar and drop left, outside the window. The bulkhead doors are unlocked, so walk out.

Take the lift downstairs and walk through the bulkhead door. Araknids wait on the other side, so be prepared. When they're out of the way, it's a clear shot to the corridor's other end and through the door.

Your goal is to get into the central dome—the dangerous-looking area behind the glass in front of you. Follow the curved corridor to the right, and go through the bulkhead door on the right side at the end. More Araknids and pods await you beyond. Clear the corridor, and go to the door at the other end.

When the door opens, hang back and take out the Araknids inside. The green canisters around the room's perimeter contain poison gas that can hurt the Araknids when the canisters are shot, but be sure you're not standing too close when the canisters explode. The green debris left behind after the explosion is also dangerous, so avoid it. When the room is clear, head to the lift on the other side (keeping an eye out for pods) and ride upstairs to the atmospherics laboratory.

The layout of the outer chamber is identical to that of the materials lab. The three bulkheads are sealed, so turn right and take the lift up to the control room. There are five control switches here. From left to right they are:

- Side Chamber Pressure Controls

- Bulkhead Lockdown Override

- Plasma Beam Controls

- Central Chamber Pressure Controls

- Side Chamber Pressure Controls

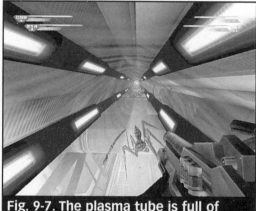
Fig. 9-7. The plasma tube is full of Light Araknids.

Activate all five switches. Take the lift down to the outer chamber. Collect the weapons, ammo, health, and energy behind the left-hand bulkhead door if you need it, then enter the central section of the lab through the middle bulkhead door. Climb onto the central dais and drop into the plasma beam tube. Crouch and proceed through the tube. Be prepared to deal with an onslaught of Light Araknids along the way (see figure 9-17).

At the end of the tube, the left hatch controls don't work, so exit to your right. Drop down the airshaft into the corridor below, where more Araknids lie in wait. More green canisters of poison gas scattered along the corridor make things interesting.

Stock up on ammo at the end of the corridor and exit through the door. The corridor beyond crawls with the usual mix of Hell aliens and more poison gas canisters. Clear the opposition, proceed to the room at the opposite end, and zap the Araknids inside. Take the lift on the room's opposite side to the biological laboratory.

The layout of the outer chamber is the same as the previous labs you've visited. The bulkheads are sealed—and that's for the best at the moment. Take the lift to the control room.

There are five switches on the control panel. Four of them open cages in the lab's left section. If you activate these switches, the caged animals (which you'll recognize as local specimens if you explored the planet's surface in Part I) run to the central lab and into the beam, growing to enormous size. They don't present a problem (no matter what size they are), but there's no need to free them.

Instead, press the bulkhead lockdown override button, descend to the lab level, and enter the right lab. Take out any Araknids in the room, then blast any that you see through the hole in the floor. When the corridor under the room looks clear, drop through the hole. Be on the lookout for additional Araknids in the corridor, and expect others to drop in through the hole if you linger in the area.

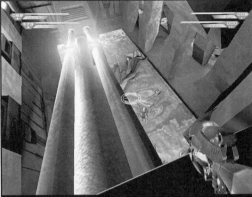

Fig. 9-18. Take out the Araknids in the pipe room from above rather than getting caught in a firefight while walking down the pipes.

There's only one direction you can go. When you come to the pipe room (see figure 9-18), take out the Araknids before walking down the pipes.

At the bottom of the pipe, jump over the side (the water isn't deep or poisonous) and take out any remaining creatures. A couple more poison gas canisters are in the area, so watch where you shoot. Search the water for ammunition and weapons before proceeding to the walkway that bisects the water. Follow the walkway—there's only one direction you can go. Watch for pods.

The source of the ion beam and the artifact you need to retrieve are at the far end of the walkway through the broken wall. You must shut down the beam to get the artifact. A Heavy Araknid lurks inside (see figure 9-19). It drops in from the catwalk above when you enter the room.

The Heavy Araknid has multiple ranged attacks that can cause serious harm (see Chapter 4 for details). The worst of these is its pod-scattering attack. The creature creates pods all over the room. These pods hatch into Light Araknids and, if the Light Araknids get into the beam, they turn into Medium Araknids. You soon face a huge onslaught of enemies in a firefight the likes of which you haven't encountered before.

Fig. 9-19. Your ultimate opponent in the bowels of Hell.

Keep moving and concentrate your fire on the Heavy Araknid. Don't get your back against the wall—the Heavy Araknid pins you there and you are dead if you can't break free. Get rid of pods when the Heavy Araknid deposits them. The more of them that hatch, the hairier things get.

You can't break the cover on the beam controls but, when you kill the Heavy Araknid, its death shriek breaks the cover for you. When this happens, deactivate the beam. Jump onto the platform and grab the artifact to end your tenure in Hell.

Tip

Health, energy, and ammunition are scattered throughout the room, mostly near and/or behind the pipes and pillars around the room's perimeter. You'll need all of it before the battle with the Heavy Araknid is over.

Back on the *Atlantis*

When you get to the ship, converse with Aida and follow her to the briefing room. Have Aida set things up and activate the keyboard to talk to Sector Commander Hawkins. He gives you some background on the artifacts, and informs you that the marines have temporarily reinstated you and the crew.

Tip

To get background information on the various facets of the game—the corporations, the Skaarj, the TCA, and so on—go to the bridge and talk to Ne'Ban before heading out on your next mission. Run through the discussion topics available and you'll learn a lot.

After you're offline with Hawkins, talk to Aida to get the briefing for your next mission—your first as a reinstated marine officer.

Visit Isaak before you go to the drop room to get a briefing on Aida's 50-caliber Pistol, Grace, as well as some background on the Izanagi Mercenaries, the so-called "Ghost Warriors," that you're about to face in the upcoming mission.

Chapter 10: Acheron

As you learned from Aida's briefing, Acheron is a unique planet that's covered by a giant life-form that the Izanagi Corporation's terraforming operation is slowly killing.

That operation stopped several days ago, and it's believed that the corporation has found another artifact. Your assignment is to infiltrate the operation and assess the situation. The Izanagi goons are getting ready to extract the artifact by force, and you have to beat them to it.

Mission Objectives:

- EXTRACT THE ARTIFACT FROM THE IZANAGI TERRAFORMING OPERATION.
- FIND A WAY DOWN INTO THE DIG SITE.
- FIND THE ARTIFACT IN THE DIG SITE.
- ARM ALL THREE DETONATORS.
- GET THE ARTIFACT.
- ESCAPE BACK TO YOUR DROPSHIP WITH THE ARTIFACT.

Outside the Terraforming Plant

Your drop ship is detected on the way in, so expect some company. Hold your ground and wait for the first Izanagi to approach, then take him out when he's in range.

Tip

Grab the weapons and ammo off the corpses. You can always use more.

Move toward the terraforming plant, but stay off the road. You're an easy target if you approach in the open. The rock formations along the road's right side provide cover. Don't stray too close to the cliff's edge and fall to your death.

Watch for flying explosives as you approach the main entrance—the Izanagi guards wield grenade and rocket launchers. Several guards are hidden on and near the construction vehicle in front of the entrance. Approach with caution and take them out using the surrounding rocks for cover.

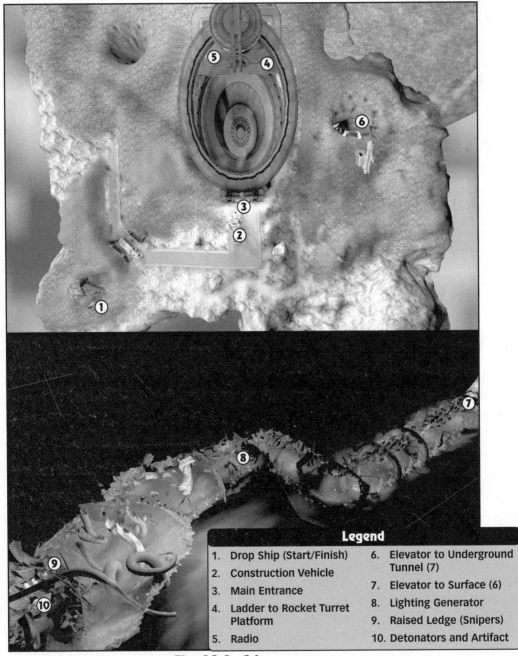

Legend

1. Drop Ship (Start/Finish)
2. Construction Vehicle
3. Main Entrance
4. Ladder to Rocket Turret Platform
5. Radio
6. Elevator to Underground Tunnel (7)
7. Elevator to Surface (6)
8. Lighting Generator
9. Raised Ledge (Snipers)
10. Detonators and Artifact

Fig. 10-1. Acheron map

After you eliminate the outside enemies, another group arrives topside and streams through the main entrance (see figure 10-2). A couple of well-placed Frag Grenades can take them out before they exit the structure. Run inside and get the health, energy, and ammo before you move on.

Fig. 10-2. A new group of enemies arrives from below when you finish off the ones stationed outside.

Tip

One of the Izanagi you take out in front of the building has a Rocket Launcher that is handy for this mission. Find it and pick it up.

Follow the walkway around the building's right side, remaining close to the wall. When you round the corner and see the large, steaming vent, slow down. A Rocket Turret is on the platform to the right of the building on the other side of the vent. If you approach in the open from the right, it

Fig. 10-3. You risk injury from the Rocket Turret if you don't destroy it before it opens fire.

detects you and opens fire when you're halfway around the vent (see figure 10-3). Use the Rocket Launcher to destroy it before you proceed to the building. There is another Izanagi guard off to the right near the crane. Take him out if he starts shooting at you.

Climb the ladder onto the Rocket Turret platform. Some Izanagi wait up there, so lob Frag Grenades to clear the way. Move left around the central structure and take care of the Izanagi on the other side. Look for the health station (and use it if necessary). Next to it is a radio. Pick it up and use it.

After the cutscene (which shows some Izanagi coming up from a pit on an elevator), go to the ladder you ascended to reach the platform. From here, you can see the pit in question—which is actually an orifice that leads into the guts of the planet-sized alien. Climb down from the platform, pick off the Izanagi the you saw in the cutscene, and proceed to the pit. Step onto the elevator and descend to the shaft's bottom. Avoid any smaller pits you see on the way (the ones with teeth)—if you fall into them, you take a great deal of damage.

Fig. 10-4. The three detonators are attached to the orb on the floor.

Moments after starting down the tunnel, you encounter Izanagi. Take them out and continue. Look for additional guards as you proceed. Check high and low—not all Izanagi troops are on the ground. Use the uneven terrain and protrusions for cover.

You'll come to a nonfunctional lighting generator with a crate, ammo, and health pickups next to it. You're now about halfway to the end of the tunnel. Just beyond you receive your new objective: "Arm all three detonators." You must deal with additional enemies in this area before moving on, so stay alert.

When you see more mine equipment and boxes, the shooting is about to start. Look up and to your left—the Izanagi goons like to snipe from the platform there. Find health and energy stations on this platform.

The three detonators are attached to the glowing orb on the floor (see figure 10-4). Arm them and get out of the way.

After the explosion, grab the artifact (which sits in the depression that held the orb you blew up) and run to the elevator. The explosion wakes up the creature, and it starts to fight. Avoid the flying orbs; they are spores that flock to you and cause damage when they make contact (see figure 10-5). Shoot them before they get close.

Watch for the green ooze flowing from the walls. This liquid is the creature's digestive fluid. Contact causes damage, so avoid the flow. When you come to a pool of fluid on the floor, move past on the ledges above the affected areas (see figure 10-6).

You encounter a few Izanagi goons along the way. Don't worry about them—between the spores and the digestive juices, they're too busy to worry about you.

When you step onto the elevator, it returns you to the surface. Make a beeline for your drop ship, avoiding the green gas and liquid geysers that spew from cracks in the ground. When you reach the ship, you encounter an Izanagi who's trying to escape. Take him out and walk to the drop ship to end the mission.

Fig. 10-5. Shoot the spores before they make contact.

Fig. 10-6. Move along the ledges lining the tunnel's side to avoid the pools of digestive fluid.

Back on the *Atlantis*

This time, you don't get to dawdle aboard the *Atlantis* between missions. In a cutscene, Aida fills you in on the situation your incursion on Acheron has created, and you're off to your next assignment.

Chapter 11: Severnaya

Your incursion on Acheron has caused massive repercussions, resulting in an Izanagi uprising on Severnaya. A squad of marines tried to destroy the dam that provides power to the Izanagi installation on the planet, but they failed and were cut off. Two men are stranded there, and it's up to you to locate and rescue them.

Mission Objectives:

- MAKE CONTACT WITH SURVIVING MARINES.
- SAVE THE MARINES FROM THE ATTACKING MERCENARIES.
- INFILTRATE THE DAM.
- FIND AND ARM THE FIRST EXPLOSIVE CHARGE.
- FIND AND ARM THE SECOND EXPLOSIVE CHARGE.
- FIND AND ARM THE THIRD EXPLOSIVE CHARGE.
- ESCAPE BACK TO YOUR DROPSHIP.

Severnaya Waterfront

The marines are pinned down by a number of Izanagi behind the hills to the right of your starting position. The only approach is a direct one. You can get close to their position by swimming there, but you can't climb out of the water near them. Use the hilly terrain as cover as you approach.

As soon as the marines are in sight, one of them gets killed (there's no way to prevent it). After you take out the Izanagi pinning the marines down, the second marine approaches you and gives you a situation report. Send him

Fig. 11-2. Make the approach to the dam safer by eliminating the outdoor sentries with the Sniper Rifle.

on his way and take over his mission—the destruction of the dam. Scour the area where the marines were hiding for weapons and equipment. Pick up the EMP Grenades that the live marine leaves behind. Also pick up the Sniper Rifle that belonged to his dead buddy—it makes your mission a lot easier.

Your first task is to infiltrate the dam. Follow the ridge to an area above the water, bearing right from the marines' position. Use the Sniper Rifle to take out the Izanagi patrolling in front of the dam from long-distance (see figure 11-2), then continue up the ridge and toward the dam. Stay close to the face of the dam as you approach—additional Izanagi are stationed in the central windows above the main entrance door. Take them out with the Sniper Rifle if you can get a clear shot without putting yourself in the line of fire. Killing them now saves you effort later.

Legend

1. Drop Ship (Start/Finish)
2. Marines
3. Snipers (Inside Dam)
4. Main Dam Entrance
5. Waterfall Entrance (to 6)
6. Waterfall Entrance Interior (Lower Level)
7. First Detonator (Middle Level)
8. Grate to Security Office
9. Security Office
10. Second Detonator
11. Turbine
12. Corridor to Sniper Position (Upper Level)
13. Corridor to Main Entrance (Middle Level)
14. Third Detonator (Behind Turbine)

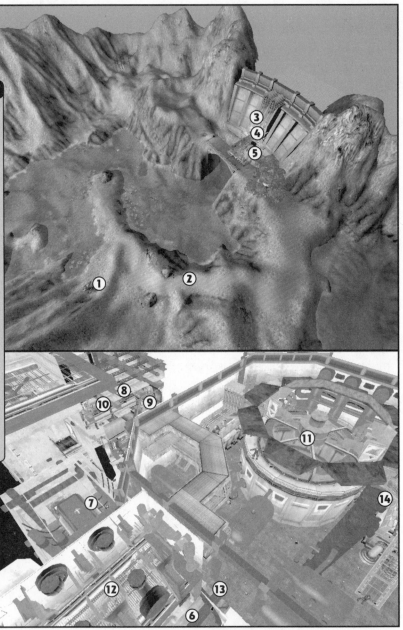

Fig. 11-1. Severnaya Waterfront map

The main door in the center of the dam is sealed, so don't bother with it. Follow the narrow walkway on the face of the dam and take the ladder down to the ground below. Staying close to the dam (and taking care not to fall over the edge of the cliff), head for the waterfall issuing from the center of the dam. Approach the opening cautiously—the area inside is patrolled, and there's an Auto Turret on the bridge spanning the river. Without entering the water, edge out and use the Rocket Launcher to blast the Auto Turret. Afterward, eliminate the patrolling Izanagi.

When the coast is clear, step into the water and run inside. Don't stop moving, or the current will carry you over the waterfall! Go past the back end of the platforms and turn right. Climb the ladder onto the right-hand platform.

Cross the bridge and head through the door on the other side. As soon as you step through, you are detected and the door shuts behind you. Continue through the door on the other side of the room, and turn left before you reach the stairs. Walk into the vent in the corner and continue through into the narrow corridor beyond. Turn around and blast the Izanagi who respond to the alarm through the vent opening before you continue.

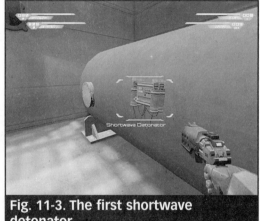

Fig. 11-3. The first shortwave detonator.

Climb the ladder at the end of the corridor. The first of three shortwave detonators is mounted on a tank at the top of the ladder (see figure 11-3). Arm it.

When you turn around (with the first detonator behind you) you see a metal girder leading up. A ladder is attached to the other side of the girder. Climb up, cross the catwalk above (crouching under the pipe to do so), turn left, and climb the ladder to the next level. Proceed along another catwalk and up another ladder, and you emerge in a crawlspace in the ceiling above a security office.

Crouch and move to the first grate. Open the grate and blast the Izanagi below. The fastest and safest method is to lob a couple of Frag Grenades in before the room's occupants look up and see you (see figure 11-4). When the coast is clear, drop down into the room.

Go to the control panel and use the central keyboard to unlock the doors. Open the lockers along the wall and stock up on health, ammo, and energy. When you're ready, head through the door at the end of the room (*not* the one on the side wall).

Fig. 11-4. Use the Grenade Launcher to clear the security office before you (literally) drop in.

Tip

When you enter the dam turbine room, don't just look for enemies on the catwalk—check the room below as well.

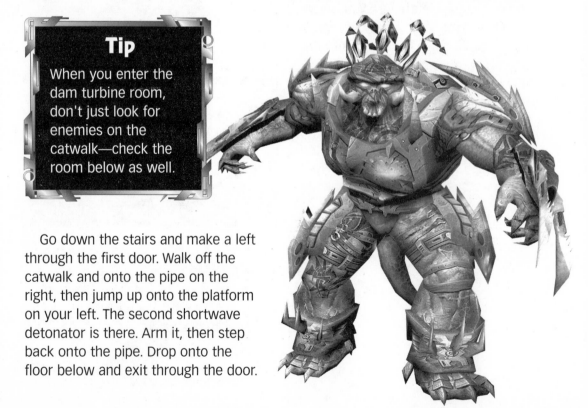

Go down the stairs and make a left through the first door. Walk off the catwalk and onto the pipe on the right, then jump up onto the platform on your left. The second shortwave detonator is there. Arm it, then step back onto the pipe. Drop onto the floor below and exit through the door.

Turn left and enter the lower level of the turbine room. Enter the room cautiously. Stay by the doorway and eliminate any enemies you spot.

The path to the left is blocked, so proceed right cautiously, hugging the black tanks ahead of you. When you get to an opening, head deeper into the room, toward the turbine. There's a security forcefield to your right and, when you get far enough inside, another springs up to cut off your retreat. In addition to any human patrols in the area, there is an Auto

Fig. 11-5. The Auto Turret pins you down shortly after you're trapped by the security forcefields. Take it out quickly!

Turret on the catwalk above, to the right of the turbine (see figure 11-5). Use the Rocket Launcher or EMP Grenades to destroy the turret as quickly as you can. Use whatever cover is available to minimize your injuries.

After you deal with the Izanagi and the Auto Turret, fire an EMP Grenade into the forcefield at the bottom of the ramp. Go up the ramp and follow the catwalk around the perimeter of the turbine, watching for enemies on the platform across the room to your left. Descend the ramp on the opposite side. Take out the Auto Turret in the alcove to the left, and turn toward the back of the room. A forcefield

blocks the corridor that leads behind the turbine. Use an EMP Grenade on it, then deal with the Izanagi beyond (if he isn't taken out in the blast that destroys the forcefield).

Before you traverse the short corridor, bounce Grenades down the corridor so that they explode at the opposite end. Another Auto Turret hides there, and it's best to disable it before you step into its line of fire (see figure 11-6).

Fig. 11-6. Before you head down the short corridor, bounce some Grenades behind the turbine to eliminate the hidden Auto Turret.

Against the back wall of the room is a series of pipes that looks like a staircase. Position yourself in front of the bottom pipe and keep jumping and moving forward until you're on the top pipe. Walk along this pipe until you reach the other end, and descend to the floor on the other side in the same manner.

The third shortwave detonator is to your right, on the backside of the turbine. Arm it and get ready to run. You now have five minutes to exit the dam before the charges blow.

Just to the left of the detonator is a stair step arrangement of three pipes. This is the most direct route out of the room. Jump up the pipes and crouch through the opening at the top. Run toward the forcefield and disable it with an EMP Grenade. More Izanagi are streaming into the room by this time, and if you time your blast right you can take out one or two when the forcefield goes. Eliminate any additional resistance quickly, and then head out the door.

Tip

Unless you have no alternative, don't pause to engage any enemies on your way out of the dam. Aida keeps you up to date on the ongoing countdown, and the five minutes passes quickly. You need to get back to the drop ship before time runs out.

The main entrance to the dam is directly ahead. Open the door and make an immediate left. Enemies shoot at you from above, but don't stop to fight unless you're close to death and you can't take a few shots in the back. Head for the down-ladder and descend to the path below. Taking care not to fall over the cliff, run up the hill and retrace your original entry path back to the drop ship. Run up to the ship to end the mission.

Enjoy the explosive show as the dam goes up in smoke. You earned it.

Back on the *Atlantis*

The *Atlantis* is experiencing some technical difficulties, and you are forced to land to effect repairs. When you take control of the scene, get your briefing from Ne'Ban, and head over to Isaak's for more info on the artifacts and on the Seagoat creature that damaged the ship. He can also fill you in on the operational details of the Sniper Rifle and Rocket Launcher.

When you're ready, head to the drop room. The drop ship isn't docked, so head through the room and down the ramp to start the next mission.

Chapter 12: Kalydon

The *Atlantis* has set down at Military Outpost Kilo Five Seven on Kalydon for repairs. The ship lands behind a shield wall, but Liandri Angel Mercenaries are expected in short order—and that means trouble. Your job is to hold down the fort long enough for Isaak to complete the ship's repairs.

Mission Objectives:

- FIND THE CACHE OF DEFENSIVE EQUIPMENT.
- SET UP DEFENSES TO PREPARE FOR ENEMY ASSAULT.
- DEFEND THE WALL UNTIL ISAAK REPAIRS THE *ATLANTIS*.

Outside the Repair Facility

When you arrive on the surface, Isaak briefs you on two new types of equipment—Plasma Field Generators and Rocket Turrets. These devices will help you hold off the enemies. To pick up these items, step up to them, and tap the Use control. To deploy them, select the item as you would a weapon and tap your Primary Fire control. Play around with the equipment to get the hang of placing it and picking it up. When you're comfortable with the equipment's operation, pick up the turret and generators. For detailed information on Plasma Field Generators and Rocket Turrets, see Chapter 3.

Your first task is to find a cache of defensive equipment that was dropped in the wrong area. There are two ways to get there:

- Head down the long canyon to your right, away from the building. When you reach what appears to be the end of the canyon, bear left and follow the path into the hills. The cache of equipment is over the ridge in a small valley (see figure 12-2).

Fig. 12-2. The defensive equipment cache (approaching from the canyon on the right).

Legend
1. Start
2. Long Canyon
3. Rock Arch
4. Equipment Container

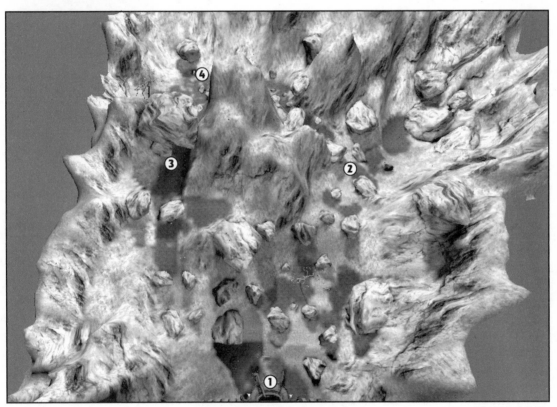

Fig. 12-1. Kalydon map

- Head into the hills on your left, following the only available path. At the top of the hill, you come to a rock arch (see figure 12-3). Move through the arch to see the equipment container in the valley.

When you grab the equipment—more Rocket Turrets and Plasma Field Generators—you trigger a countdown to the arrival of the first wave of Liandri Angels, whose ship arrives at the end of the long canyon farthest from the building.

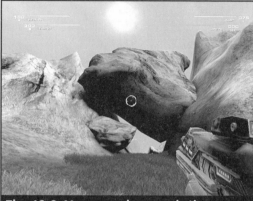

Fig. 12-3. You can also reach the equipment cache by climbing into the hills on your left and passing through this arch.

Note

Four waves of Liandri arrive in this mission. The arrival of each successive wave is triggered by the eradication of the wave before it. Despite the fact that you are providing time for your crew to complete repairs on the *Atlantis*, time has little to do with it. No matter how long the fighting lasts, the mission doesn't end until most of the fourth wave of Liandri is defeated.

Leave the valley where the defensive cache is stored via the path through the rock arch. Set up two Plasma Field Generators and one Rocket Turret to block the path through the arch on your way out (see figure 12-4).

Fig. 12-4. Set your defenses at the arch prior to the first Liandri incursion.

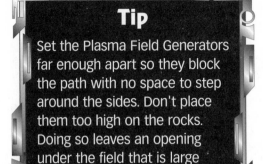

Tip

Set the Plasma Field Generators far enough apart so they block the path with no space to step around the sides. Don't place them too high on the rocks. Doing so leaves an opening under the field that is large enough to move through.

Proceed to the mouth of the long canyon on the building's side, and create a defensive perimeter. Set up the remaining Plasma Field Generators to block the canyon path, and set the two remaining Rocket Turrets on opposite sides of the canyon, on high positions that give them a clear field of fire up the canyon away from the building (see figure 12-5).

The first wave of Liandri Angels is in sight. Your automated defenses should take out a good number of the intruders, but pick off as many Angels as you can to prevent them from damaging the Plasma Field Generators and Rocket Turrets. Your ammo is limited in this mission, so make every shot count.

Fig. 12-5. Set up a perimeter at the mouth of the canyon on the building end, with the Rocket Turrets up high to provide a good field of fire.

Caution

Most of the Liandri Angels are easy to deal with, but the Heavy Angels have a lot of protection and their armor allows them to fly! When one of these Angels is nearby, make her your primary target.

When the last member of the first Liandri attack force is killed, the next wave arrives. The second wave sets down in the valley where you retrieved the defensive cache and moves toward the building through the rock arch. Move into the hills to a position where you can watch the attack (see figure 12-6). The more Liandri you shoot, the longer the defenses hold.

Fig. 12-6. Take up a sheltered position near the arch to deal with the second wave of Liandri.

Caution

When firing toward your automated defenses, avoid using high explosives (rockets and Frag Grenades). These weapons, carelessly targeted, can damage or destroy your Plasma Field Generators and Rocket Turrets.

When the second wave is wiped out, grab the Rocket Turret in the arch (if it hasn't been destroyed). Head toward the building and take up a sheltered position away from your defenses in the long canyon (see figure 12-7). The third wave arrives in the canyon within a minute.

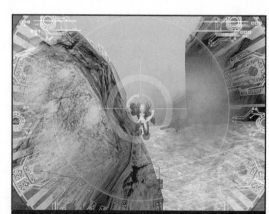

Fig. 12-7. Take a sheltered position behind the long canyon defenses to deal with the third wave of Liandri.

After dealing with wave three, grab any remaining nearby Rocket Turrets. Retreat toward the concrete barrier in front of the building, setting up Rocket Turrets so they face the tall rock formation that bisects the long canyon and the path to the rock arch. Take a position behind the concrete barrier and wait for wave four to arrive. They land on top of the rock formation (see figure 12-8).

Fig. 12-8. The fourth wave of Angels arrives.

Stay behind the barrier, and pick off any Angels that get past the Rocket Turrets. Watch your left flank to make sure none of your enemies runs around the rocks there.

Eventually, Isaak pronounces the repairs to the *Atlantis* complete and opens the building door behind you. Run through the door to end the mission. If any Liandri remain, watch for incoming fire on your way.

Note

If Liandri Angels remain after Isaak says the ship is ready to leave, you don't have to kill them to complete the mission.

Back on the *Atlantis*

When you return to the ship, you don't get a chance to wander around. Commander Hawkins fills you in on the next mission in a cutscene, then you're off to Sulferon.

Chapter 13: Sulferon

A secret Izanagi facility on Sulferon has developed a tool to detect alien artifacts like the ones you recovered in previous missions, and the marines want it. Your orders are to infiltrate the Sulferon facility and retrieve data on the artifact-detecting tool.

Mission Objectives:

- CLEAR THE BASE AND SURROUNDING AREA OF ALL ENEMY FORCES.
- OBTAIN THE IMPORTANT DATA FROM THE INSTALLATION'S COMPUTER SYSTEM.
- DEACTIVATE THE DISTRESS CALL.
- PROTECT THE TECHNICIAN UNTIL HE CAN RETRIEVE THE INFORMATION FROM THE DAMAGED COMPUTER.
- DESTROY ALL ATTACKING FORCES.

Part I: Secret Izanagi Facility

Note the Izanagi patrols and defenses in the opening cutscene. Your first task is to approach the base and take them out, so learn what you're up against.

Cross the landing pad to the first sand dune that lies between you and the base. Use the scope on the Sniper Rifle to look at the base. Two Rocket Turrets are visible from this angle (see figure 13-2). Remember their positions.

Fig. 13-2. Getting the lay of the land. Note the Rocket Turrets along the base wall, one on each side of the bones in this image.

Stay low, turn left, and move parallel to the sand dune. A couple of Izanagi patrol this area. Using the bones and crates in the area for cover, take them out.

Move toward the building and use the terrain features as cover. Pause from time to time and use the Sniper Rifle scope to search the horizon for additional Izanagi troops. Pop them from a distance, keeping in mind that your Sniper Rifle ammo is extremely limited. The Izanagi patrols are heavily armored, so it takes a couple of Sniper Rifle shots (or a well-placed head shot) to put them down.

Legend	
1. Landing Pad (Start)	6. Lower Control Room (Inside, Lower Level)
2. Outer Wall	
3. Inner Wall	7. Upper Control Room (Inside, Upper Level)
4. Courtyard	
5. Front Door	8. "Back Door" (Side of Building, Lower Level)

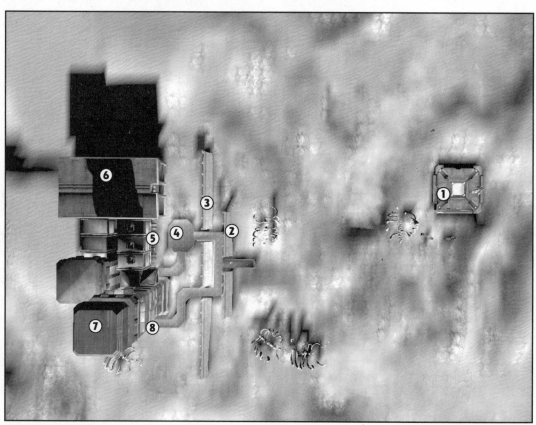

Fig. 13-1. Sulferon map

The Rocket Turrets can detect you as soon as you reach the far side of the smoking crater adjacent to the landing site. Stay low in the crater until you're ready, and then run toward the pile of bones that lies between you and the building. Stay mobile and use the Rocket or Grenade Launcher to take out both turrets (see figure 13-3).

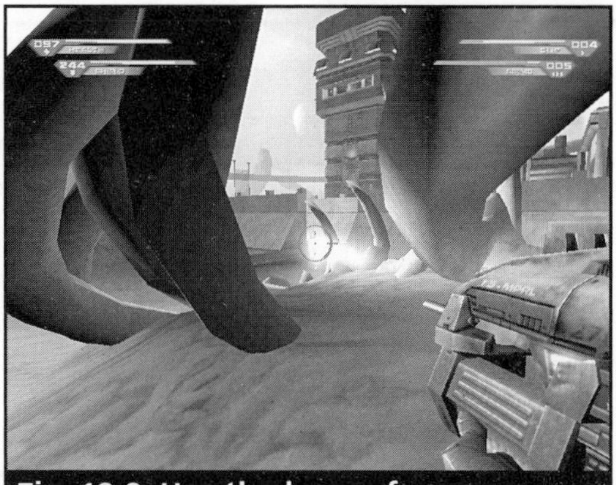

After the turrets are disabled, move in from the right, past the wreckage of the right-hand turret, and turn left into the space between the outer and inner walls. Turn right and enter the courtyard through the first opening in the inner wall.

Fig. 13-3. Use the bones for cover while you blast the Rocket Turrets.

Shortly after you step through the opening, you're spotted, and the Izanagi trigger a distress signal. Use the wall for cover and take out any Izanagi milling about the courtyard from long range. (Hopefully, you still have a few rounds remaining in the Sniper Rifle.) When the coast is clear, cross the courtyard and enter through the front door. If you are spotted in the courtyard, the Izanagi might trigger a distress call. They eventually trigger the distress call anyway, so don't worry about it.

Caution

Another Rocket Turret is positioned at the far end of the walkway. If you stray far beyond the first opening in the inner wall, it fires on you.

More Izanagi are inside the building, in the junction room beyond the stairs. There are also three Auto Turrets. The one visible from the entrance fires at you when the door opens. Have your Grenade Launcher ready, and fire at the first turret as soon as you step inside (see figure 13-4). Lob the grenades high so they reach the top of the far staircase—direct hits are more effective.

Fig. 13-4. Use the Grenade Launcher to destroy the first turret as soon as you step into the building.

Check the corridors to the left and right for additional Izanagi before walking downstairs. Don't bother with either of these corridors for the time being.

The second and third Auto Turrets are in the junction room's back-right and front-left corners. When you start down the stairs, the rear one fires at you. Use the Grenade Launcher to put it out of commission. Bounce a couple of grenades around the corner to your left to knock out the third turret before ascending the steps.

There are more Izanagi in the junction room, and reinforcements file in from the corridors to the right and left. Prepare for them.

With your back to the stairs, turn right and go through the door. Expect additional Izanagi in the corridor beyond, and watch your back—reinforcements might arrive from that direction as well. Clear the corridor and proceed through the next door. Deal with more Izanagi forces in the room beyond and take the ammo, energy, and health scattered around the room. During the battle, one of the Izanagi blows the control panel. This is inevitable, so don't worry about it.

Exit the room using the second door (the one you didn't enter through). In the corridor beyond, just behind the stacked crates, is another Auto Turret. It faces the other direction, so you're safe. Edge out from behind the crates and use the Dispersion Pistol to destroy the turret. (It takes many shots with this weapon, but using it conserves other scarce ammunition.) When you destroy the turret, proceed through the door at the opposite end.

You should recognize where you are now. Walk forward down the corridor, past the door through which you entered the building, and proceed to the room at the far end. Deal with any Izanagi troops, then board the lift and ascend to the level above.

Your goal now is to deactivate the distress call. At the top of the lift, turn left or right to reach the control room. Either way, expect to encounter Izanagi guards. Eliminate them. Collect the weapons and ammo against the wall opposite the control console before you deactivate the transmission switch in the center of the console (see figure 13-5).

If the mission doesn't end when the distress call is deactivated, there are still enemies remaining. Search the base inside and out, and eliminate everything that moves. When all enemies are eliminated and the message is shut down, the next phase of the mission begins.

Fig. 13-5. Clear the floor of enemies and collect the available weapons and ammo. Deactivate the distress call.

Part II: Defend

A marine ship drops off a technician to retrieve the data you came for and a group of marines to help you defend him.

The first of three ships full of Izanagi Ghost Warriors arrives a little over a minute after the mission begins (watch the countdown). Deploy your marines immediately (step up and talk to them to give them orders). Deploy the marines as follows (in the order shown):

Note

The "back door" is on the side of the building (the left side as you face the main entrance from the outside).

- **Lt. Cosner:** guard the front wall

- **Lt. Caruso:** guard the front door

- **PFC Taba:** guard the back door

- **Sgt. Easley:** guard the control room

Pick up all available ammo and weapons, and pump up your health and energy as far as you can before heading out the front door. Assume a position outside the door and grab your Sniper Rifle. Now, sit back and wait for your enemies to come to you.

Tip

If all goes well, you should be able to eliminate the Izanagi forces without their ever entering the base. However, if you hear Aida say that the enemy has reached the control room, go there and defend the technician.

The first Izanagi ship touches down on the pad where you landed at the start of the mission. Crouch down and wait. Watch your marines, the wall's openings, and the open spaces at the wall's ends. When the Izanagi arrive, let your marines engage at close range while you watch through the Sniper Rifle scope (see figure 13-6). Shoot every enemy that comes into your sights. If your marines are overwhelmed, you can move in and help, but it's safer to stay near the building and cover the front entrance.

Caution

Be careful not to shoot your own marines in the heat of battle. Besides the enraged screams your allies raise when you shoot them, you can tell combatants apart by their armor. Izanagi Ghost Warrior armor has red highlights, and marine armor is all black.

Fig. 13-6. Use the Sniper Rifle to help the marines without wading headlong into the fray.

After you eliminate most of the first group, a second ship arrives (see figure 13-7). This one lands closer, outside the walls. Hold your position at the door and continue picking off Ghost Warriors. Watch your flanks, especially to the right, to make sure no enemies circle the building and assault the other entrance.

Wave three arrives when most of wave two has been eliminated. They land behind the building and head for the back door. When the courtyard is secure, turn right and run to the end of the building. Crouch at the corner and turn right to get a view of the building's side. Use the Sniper Rifle to assist the marine covering the door in eliminating the incoming Izanagi (see figure 13-8). The Ghost Warriors approach both from behind the sand dunes and behind the bones to the left, so keep your eyes open.

Fig. 13-7. The second enemy ship lands much closer to the building.

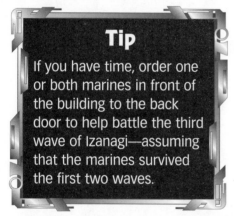

Tip

If you have time, order one or both marines in front of the building to the back door to help battle the third wave of Izanagi—assuming that the marines survived the first two waves.

Fig. 13-8. Watch the dunes behind the building for the third wave of Ghost Warriors, and pick them off as they break cover.

When you have eliminated all three waves of Izanagi, the technician finishes downloading the data and the mission ends.

Back on the *Atlantis*

After your conversation with Ne'Ban, go to the briefing room and have Aida fill you in on your next mission. Afterward, visit Isaak and get a briefing on your newest weapon, the SpiderGun, which Isaak has constructed using Araknid biomass recovered during the Hell mission.

When ready, go to the drop room and launch the next mission.

Chapter 14: Janus

The Izanagi and Liandri have located the Polaris research lab on Janus and are attacking the facility. They are on the ground and fortifying their positions. Most of the scientists have been evacuated, but the lead artifact researcher, Dr. Meyer, is still inside—along with two of the artifacts.

Your mission: Recover both artifacts and keep the doctor safe.

Mission Objectives:

- FIND AND OBTAIN THE TWO ARTIFACTS BEFORE YOUR ENEMIES CAN.
- ENTER THE JANUS COMPLEX.
- FIND THE LABORATORY SECTION.
- RESCUE THE SCIENTIST.
- PROTECT MEYER.
- GET BACK TO YOUR DROPSHIP.
- GET TO THE ROOF FOR EXTRACTION.
- CLEAR THE WAY TO THE LIFT ON THE OTHER SIDE OF THE BUILDING.

- TAKE MEYER UP TO THE ROOF ON THE LIFT.
- SET UP DEFENSES TO PREPARE FOR ENEMY ASSAULT.
- NOTIFY MEYER WHEN HE CAN ACTIVATE THE ANTIQUE RADIO.
- PROTECT MEYER UNTIL HE CAN CONTACT THE *ATLANTIS*.
- MEET MEYER IN THE RADIO ROOM TO CALL THE *ATLANTIS*.

Part I: Outside Polaris

Within moments of your arrival, an Izanagi stationed on the platform of the right sniper tower pelts you with rockets. To make matters worse, another Izanagi, armed with a Rocket Launcher, patrols the ground between the landing pad and the bridge.

Take cover behind the drop ship and crouch underneath it. Use the Sniper Rifle to take out the guard on the ground, then to take out the one on the tower (see figure 14-2).

Fig. 14-2. After dealing with the guard on the ground, snipe the fellow on the tower platform.

Tip

After you clear the opposition near the landing pad, climb the right tower. Health, energy, and ammunition wait for you on the platform from which the Izanagi was firing rockets. The tower makes a great vantage point for sniping the units patrolling the bridge (which is where you're headed next).

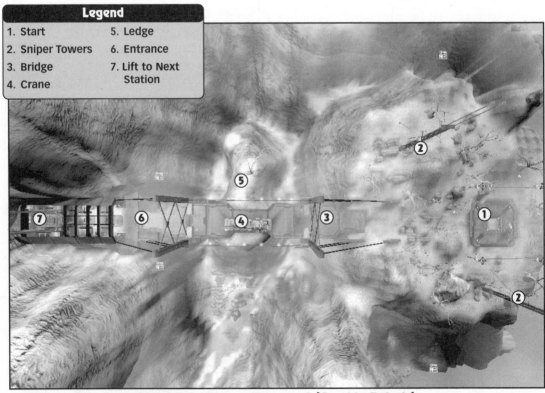

Legend

1. Start
2. Sniper Towers
3. Bridge
4. Crane
5. Ledge
6. Entrance
7. Lift to Next Station

Fig. 14-1. Janus map, part I (Outside Polaris)

Bear left from the landing platform, pick up the cache of weapons and ammo, then bear right toward the bridge. Don't stray too far left; you'll fall off a cliff.

When the troops stationed in the center of the bridge see you, they set up a pair of Plasma Field Generators and an Auto Turret to block your way. If you're fast, you can take them out before they complete their work. If not, use EMP Grenades to take out the turret and the forcefield, then deal with the human element. Several Izanagi are stationed on the bridge beyond the crane; some of them may join the fight with the first bridge group.

A Rocket Turret is on the bridge's left side, past the crane. Use your Sniper Rifle scope to see it before it sees you (see figure 14-3). Get a clear line of fire and destroy it from a distance.

As you pass the crane, look right. Izanagi hang out on a narrow stretch of land there.

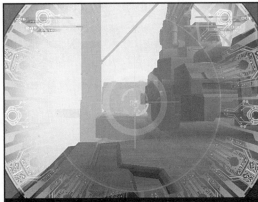

Fig. 14-3. Destroy the Rocket Turret beyond the crane before it detects you.

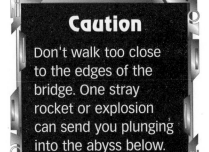

Caution

Don't walk too close to the edges of the bridge. One stray rocket or explosion can send you plunging into the abyss below.

Beyond the crane, the Izanagi erect another forcefield. Take it down using the EMP Grenades, and mop up the rest of the opposition in the vicinity (who are waiting behind the large crates to your left and right) before moving on.

The enemies inside the room at the end of the bridge aren't apparent, but they come out of hiding when you approach. Ignore the Izanagi on the ground and concentrate on the Izanagi running along the platform on the right. If given the chance, the one on the right sets up a Rocket Turret. Avoid this by taking him out first (see figure 14-4).

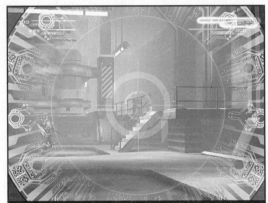

Fig. 14-4. Concentrate your fire on the enemy on the right platform to prevent him from setting up a Rocket Turret.

Tip

If the Izanagi on the platform sets up the Rocket Turret, take out the enemy on the floor, then rush the platform holding the turret, dodging rockets on the way. Crouch low in front of the stairs, and the Rocket Turret fires into the ground, destroying itself but inflicting only minimal damage upon you.

When the room is clear, climb the steps onto the platform and head left, deeper into the facility. Past the second column on your left is the cargo lift alcove. An Auto Turret guards the alcove, and you must destroy it before entering. Activate the control to open the lift door, step into the cargo lift, and start the lift to proceed to the next section of the mission.

Part II: Polaris Entrance

Legend
1. Start
2. Scientist
3. Crate Room
4. Finish

Fig. 14-5. Janus map, part II

When you step off the lift, talk to the Axon scientist to gain access to the facility. You encounter your first opposition past the third door. Expect enemy reinforcements from the corridor beyond as the battle continues.

At the end of the corridor, you'll reach a room full of crates with a glass ceiling. Assuming the Izanagi stationed there didn't come to their friends' aid in the corridor, there are mercs to deal with inside. There are also two Auto Turrets— one at the end of each of the corridors on either side of the crate that's directly in front of you when you enter the room.

Don't waste the time and ammo destroying the turrets. Turn right or left and follow the side wall to the room's far end, which you should reach without Auto Turret interference. Look for additional Izanagi Mercs hiding in the crates and at the room's opposite end.

Go through the door in the center of the far wall to proceed to the next section of the level.

Part III: Polaris Geologics Research

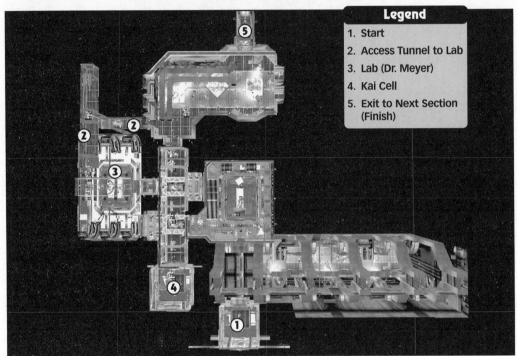

Legend
1. Start
2. Access Tunnel to Lab
3. Lab (Dr. Meyer)
4. Kai Cell
5. Exit to Next Section (Finish)

Fig. 14-6. Janus map, part III

Open the door, proceed to the room at the end of the corridor, and exit through the door on your left—but watch out! There's an Auto Turret looking you in the face when the door opens! Blast the Auto Turret, ducking in and out through the door to minimize your injuries.

Exit the room, turn right, and follow the corridor to the end. Step through the door at the end of the corridor and blast the Izanagi inside. Take out the Auto Turret in the left access tunnel before proceeding into the room (see figure 14-7).

Fig. 14-7. Destroy the Auto Turret in the access tunnel before stepping into the lab.

Gather the goodies scattered about the room. Enter the access tunnel where you destroyed the Auto Turret. Follow it to the end, take the lift to the upper level, turn left, and follow the upper tunnel as far as you can.

At the tunnel's end, a vent leads into the lab where Dr. Meyer is being tortured (see figure 14-8). Draw a bead on the scientist's captor and shoot him from above. When the coast is clear, drop into the room.

Fig. 14-8. Follow the upper tunnel to the room where Dr. Meyer is being tortured.

Once free of his captor, Dr. Meyer leads you down the hall to the room where the artifacts are locked up. Meyer refuses to give you the artifacts until you get him out of the complex. Agree to his terms. Start walking back the way you came.

Before you get far, the Liandri land and blow up the bridge outside. Aida informs you that you have to get to the roof to escape. Follow Meyer when he offers to lead the way. He leads you to the room at the corridor's opposite end, and through the door on the far side. You're off to the next section of the mission.

Part IV: Polaris Geologics Research Exterior

Follow Meyer into the control room, and open the opposite door. Izanagi lurk in the next room. Deal with them, then follow Meyer when he leaves.

The outer door is jammed, so Meyer leads you into a conference room that's crawling with Izanagi. After you clear the room, Meyer opens the window shutters and sends you outside to find and secure the maintenance rig on the other side of the building.

Step through the window onto the ledge outside and turn right. Move toward the corner. The ledge is narrow, so watch your step.

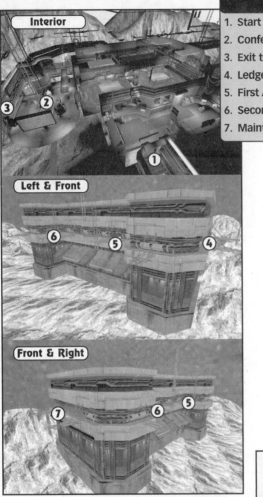

Legend
1. Start
2. Conference Room
3. Exit to Ledge (4)
4. Ledge Starting Point
5. First Auto Turret
6. Second Auto Turret
7. Maintenance Rig (Finish)

Interior

Left & Front

Front & Right

Fig. 14-9. Janus map, part IV (Polaris Geologics Research Exterior)

Enemy resistance—a group of Liandri Angels—waits around the first corner. Step out far enough for them to see you, then retreat to draw them to you (see figure 14-10). Every hit you take drives you from your attackers, so don't fight with your back to the ledge.

Fig. 14-10. Draw the Liandri around the corner and engage them with your back to the walkway, not the abyss below.

The way is clear around the next corner, but approach corner three cautiously. An Auto Turret and several additional Liandri are waiting (see figure 14-11). Draw as many of the Liandri as you can around the corner—out of the Auto Turret's field of fire—and take care of them. After you eliminate them, you can destroy the turret or run the gauntlet around the corner to your right until you're out of the turret's field of fire. When you reach the long ledge segment ahead, you're clear.

Fig. 14-11. The second group of Liandri Angels you encounter on the ledge has an Auto Turret to back it up.

Continue along the long ledge. This ledge segment has four outcroppings, the first holds the Auto Turret you ran past. Another Auto Turret awaits you on the on the fourth outcropping, behind the crate. Either destroy it or run past it and endure the pain. More Liandri Angels are around the corner past this turret.

After a couple more turns and one more Liandri encounter (watch out for the rockets), you make it to the maintenance rig (see figure 14-12).

Fig. 14-12. Your trek around the outside ledge ends when you reach the maintenance rig.

Wait on the rig until Meyer arrives. He activates the controls, and you're off to the next phase of the mission.

Part V: Polaris Geologics Research Rooftop

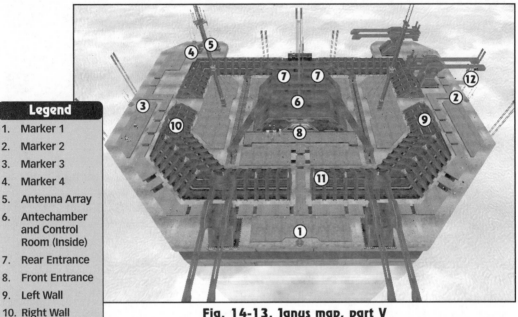

Legend
1. Marker 1
2. Marker 2
3. Marker 3
4. Marker 4
5. Antenna Array
6. Antechamber and Control Room (Inside)
7. Rear Entrance
8. Front Entrance
9. Left Wall
10. Right Wall
11. Front Wall
12. Start

Fig. 14-13. Janus map, part V

Walk to Meyer and the marine to get the situation update, then follow Meyer to the control room. Scour the room for equipment (the Plasma Field Generators stored there come in handy), then return to the rooftop. On your way out, note that the antechamber outside of the control room has three entrances—the one through which you entered and two back entrances, left and right of the stairway (see figure 14-14).

Sometime...TODAY would be nice.

Fig. 14-14. Cover the rear doors outside the control room when you set up your defenses.

Your next task is to set up a defensive perimeter to protect Meyer while he sends his transmission. You have four marines and a lot of equipment at your disposal.

Grab the equipment and weapons in the control room, then head outside. Grab the turrets and Plasma Field Generators outside the main entrance, then deploy the marines. Set their assignments as follows:

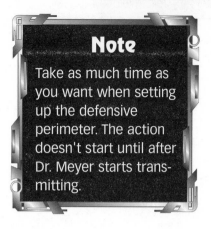

Note

Take as much time as you want when setting up the defensive perimeter. The action doesn't start until after Dr. Meyer starts transmitting.

- **Lt. Crable:** Guard the perimeter

- **Lt. Chavez:** Guard the front entrance

- **Pvt. Sadao:** Guard the right wall

- **Sgt. Harrison:** Guard the left wall

Set up your automated defenses. Deploy your equipment as follows:

- Place two Plasma Field Generators in each of the openings in the outer wall (see figure 14-15).

- Place the Rocket Turret outside the front entrance, facing the opening in the wall that leads to Marker 1.

Fig. 14-15. Block the openings in the outer walls with Plasma Field Generators.

- Place the Auto Turrets in the outer room above the control room, each facing one of the back doors.

- Place two Plasma Field Generators at the top of the stairs leading to the control room, one on either side of the stairs, and place the third in the center of the staircase at the bottom (forming a triangular forcefield that surrounds most of the stairway).

With everyone deployed and your perimeter set, you're ready to transmit. Return to the control room and talk to Meyer to set events in motion.

The first attack wave—Liandri Angels, some of the Heavy variety—arrives moments after Meyer starts transmitting. Listen to your marines when the attack begins—they call out the position of the contacts by marker number. There are four numbered markers around the rooftop outside the wall (see figure 14-16). They are:

- **Marker 1:** Outside the front wall

- **Marker 2:** Outside the left wall (as you face away from the main entrance to the building)

- **Marker 3:** Outside the right wall (as you face away from the main entrance to the building)

- **Marker 4:** Next to the antenna array near the rear of the roof, on the same side as Marker 3

Fig. 14-16. Know the position of the four numbered markers on the roof so that you can respond to threats when the marines spot them.

When your men spot an enemy, hightail it to the marker in question, and engage. Open the forcefield on that side and go outside the wall to deal with the enemies—you can't hit anything through the field. Any marines inside the wall near the entrance when you open the forcefield assist you. If they don't follow you, order them to cover you.

The second wave of attackers (more Liandri) arrives moments after the first wave is eradicated. Continue fighting until all of the enemies are eliminated. When the coast is clear, Meyer contacts you and asks you to raise the antenna array at Marker 4 (see figure 14-17). Go to the antenna and activate the controls.

Fig. 14-17. When Meyer asks you to do so, raise the antenna.

Caution

If you think you've cleared the second wave of Liandri, but you haven't received Meyer's message (and the music is still in "action" mode), check your perimeter. If one of the forcefields is down, an enemy is inside. The stairway forcefield won't hold forever, so get in there and take out the intruder before she gets to Meyer.

The next Liandri ship arrives when the antenna goes up—and it lands at Marker 3! (See figure 14-18.) Take up a defensive position near the antenna and attack when the mercs hit the platform. Use the Sniper Rifle if you have available rounds—it keeps you out of harm's way and makes fast work of this wave.

The fourth wave of mercs arrives at Marker 2. Head there and take them out, keeping them outside the wall. After you take care of this wave, another arrives between Markers 1 and 3. Order your remaining marines to cover the front and right entrances during this final wave.

After you dispose of the last of the Liandri Angels, Meyer signals that his work is done. Go to the control room to end the mission.

Fig. 14-18. The third wave of Izanagi mercs arrives after you raise the antenna.

Back on the *Atlantis*

After Hawkins informs you of your marine reinstatement, Aida expresses her concern about the situation, and tells you that Ne'Ban's people want him transferred off the *Atlantis*. Talk to Ne'Ban, then go to the briefing room and activate the hologram table to see a map of your next mission site.

To learn about the Smoke Grenade, visit Isaak. Otherwise, go to the drop room and start the next mission.

Chapter 15: Na-Koja Abad

Hawkins tells you the scientists believe the seven artifacts, when combined, form an ultra-powerful weapon. You already have five, and it is imperative that the remaining two artifacts be captured.

One of the two remaining artifacts is at an Izanagi installation and dig site on Na-Koja Abad, and that's your next destination. You must infiltrate the base and retrieve the artifact.

Mission Objectives:

- Find the alien dig site.
- Deactivate the force field.
- Infiltrate the Izanagi research facility.
- Find the bridge entrance to the alien dig site.
- Find and obtain the artifact.
- Escape the dig site with the artifact.

Part I: Na-Koja Abad

Na-Koja Abad is a foggy place, so it's easy to get turned around. Luckily, you're facing in more or less the right direction when you start the mission. Move through the valley with the drop ship behind you. Follow the line of hills on the left side of the valley, constantly bearing left, and you'll eventually come to the dig site.

There are two indigenous life-forms on the planet. The flying creatures are harmless, but watch out for the Snipes (see figure 15-2). If they get close enough, they bite—and there are enough of them around to do some serious damage.

Tip

Use your Dispersion Pistol on the Snipes. There's no need to waste precious ammunition on them.

Fig. 15-2. Some of the local fauna like to bite.

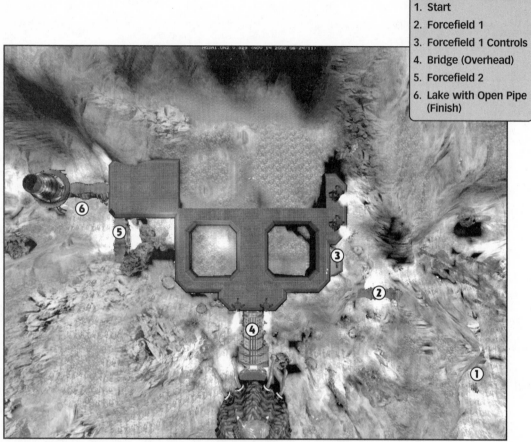

Legend
1. Start
2. Forcefield 1
3. Forcefield 1 Controls
4. Bridge (Overhead)
5. Forcefield 2
6. Lake with Open Pipe (Finish)

Fig. 15-1. Na-Koja Abad map, part I

As you approach the first forcefield, you hear a pair of Izanagi patrolling the path over the rise while discussing the artifact. Use the Sniper Rifle to get rid of them and continue along the path to the crest of the hill. Two Auto Turrets are mounted on top of the wall, one on either side of the forcefield. When you can see them clearly, take them out. It should now be safe to approach.

You need to get through the door, but a forcefield blocks your way. Don't waste EMP Grenades on it—they're ineffective. Follow the path to your right. A building just around the corner is patrolled by several Izanagi. Instead of following the main path, climb the hill to your left. There's a doorway near the left end of the structure (see figure 15-3). Take out the Izanagi in the area (look toward the other end of the building for additional enemies) and enter the building.

Fig. 15-3. The controls for shutting down the forcefield are behind this door.

Open the fuse box to your left and use the button inside to deactivate the forcefield. Help yourself to the health, energy, ammunition, and the Auto Turret stored here, and then retrace your steps back down the hill. When you reach the opening, the forcefield should be down.

Tip

You can use the Auto Turret as needed throughout the mission, but don't leave it behind or let it get destroyed. It comes in handy near the end of the mission.

Several Izanagi patrol the canyon just beyond the opening, so enter cautiously. Use the crates and natural cover to avoid enemy fire.

The next group of enemies you encounter is stationed near a bridge that spans the canyon. Instead of walking into their waiting arms, climb the hill on the right and move to a spot that overlooks their position. Snipe them from this vantage point and they'll never know what hit them (see figure 15-4). Collect the ammunition, health, and energy under the bridge before you move on.

Fig. 15-4. Take to the high ground right of the bridge and eliminate the Izanagi from above.

Continue past the bridge until you reach another forcefield gate. Turn off the forcefield and step through. Like the previous forcefield gate, this one is protected by automated defenses. There's only one Auto Turret on this end (to your right). Edge out until you can see the turret and blast it.

The area outside the gate is crawling with Snipes, so have your Dispersion Pistol ready. In the lake to your right is a pipe that leads into the building. Swim to the mouth of the pipe, and enter. Climb the ladder at the opposite end of the pipe to start the next part of the mission.

Caution

Snipes can swim. If you hear splashes while you're in the water, look around for swimming critters and blast them before they get close.

Part II: Izanagi Xeno Research Facility

Continue up the ladder and into the corridor. The door at the end is locked, so go through the vent on the right side of the corridor. Climb the ladder beyond and follow the upper corridor until you hear two scientists talking. After the conversation, round the corner and enter the lab. Jump over the railing to the lab floor and kill the Izanagi guard. There's no need to kill the scientists—they're harmless.

Legend

1. Start
2. Access Vent to First Lab
3. First Lab
4. Steam Pipe Corridor
5. Second Lab (Takkras)
6. Ammo Corridor
7. Large Storage Room
8. Third Lab
9. Lift to Next Section (Finish)

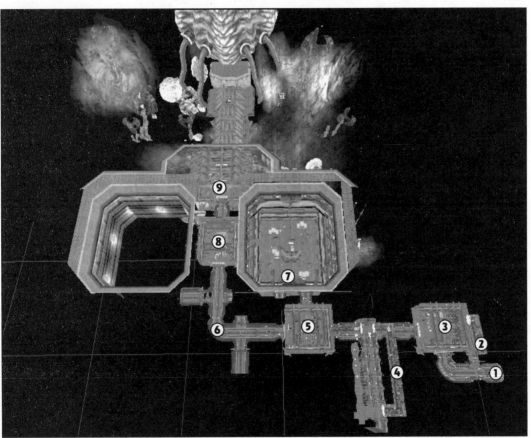

Fig. 15-5. Na-Koja Abad map, part II

Two doors lead out of the room. The one opposite the holograms just leads back to the corridor where you entered the complex, so exit the lab through the other door.

The door at the opposite end of the corridor is locked so don't bother with it. Go to the opening on the left side of the corridor and jump onto one of the ledges that run along the sides. Follow the ledge to the opposite end, and climb the ladder in the center of the shaft. As you traverse the ledge, time

Fig. 15-6. Avoid the jets of steam as you move through the pipe shaft.

your passage so that you don't get burned by the steam (see figure 15-6).

Upstairs, enter the corridor. Around the first corner to the left (at the far end of the corner) is an Auto Turret. Fire a couple of rockets down the hallway to destroy it. You're within the turret's range when you step around the corner, so don't spend time lining up your shots.

Continue down the corridor until you reach a catwalk that looks down on another lab. Once again, two scientists are in the midst of an experiment. This one goes a little awry, and the Izanagi guard shoots one of the scientists. Eliminate the guard from above, collect the health and energy on the catwalk (if you need it) and jump over the railing to the floor.

Take the Takkras from the lab table. (For info on Takkras, see Chapter 3.) If you kill the guard before the experiment goes awry, there are three Takkras on the table—otherwise there are only two. Three exits are available. The one on the end of the room closest to the Takkra table leads to the pipe shaft. The one at the opposite end of the room leads to a long corridor full of locked doors, ammo, and health stashes. Stock up in the corridor and return to the lab.

Tip

No matter how tempted you might be to use the Takkras, hold on to them. They come in handy near the end of the mission.

Exit the lab through the third door (the one directly opposite the hologram). This opens into a room with a large structure dominating the center (see figure 15-7). Izanagi guard the catwalk you enter upon and the floor below. You can't retreat to the lab (the door locks behind you) so deal with the enemies as quickly as possible. Explosive canisters are scattered throughout the room, both upstairs and down. Stay clear of them during the firefight.

Fig. 15-7. This room is your destination after exiting the second lab.

An Auto Turret is hidden in an alcove along the right wall (which also contains a ladder leading to the floor below). Health and energy stations lie beyond the turret, so eliminate this threat to take advantage of the rewards.

Enter the central structure via the catwalk opposite the Auto Turret alcove and climb the ladder. Cross the catwalk to enter the lab. Eliminate the Izanagi and jump down into the lab. Once again there are three exits, two of which lead back to areas you've already explored. Head through door number three (the one behind the target wall that was being blasted in the experiment) and through the corridor beyond.

Tip

A few pick-ups are available downstairs, so it might be worth jumping down and exploring. Near the wall below the door you entered is a "suspicious crate" with a flashing red beacon on it. There's nothing inside but one of the Snipes you encountered outside, so there's no need to open it.

Izanagi patrol on the other side of the door at the far end. Step through and end their shift. Ride the lift in the center of the platform to the level below.

Stock up on ammo, health, and energy, and then exit through the only available door. Follow the corridor, head through the next door, and activate the lift inside to go to the next part of the mission.

Part III: Excavation

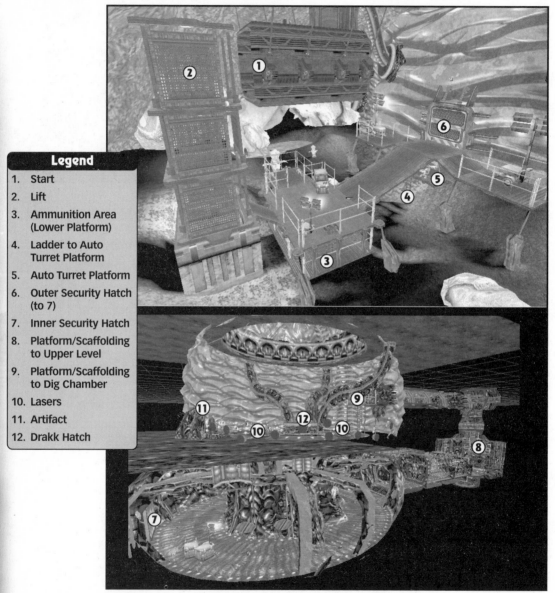

Legend

1. Start
2. Lift
3. Ammunition Area (Lower Platform)
4. Ladder to Auto Turret Platform
5. Auto Turret Platform
6. Outer Security Hatch (to 7)
7. Inner Security Hatch
8. Platform/Scaffolding to Upper Level
9. Platform/Scaffolding to Dig Chamber
10. Lasers
11. Artifact
12. Drakk Hatch

Fig. 15-8. Na-Koja Abad map, part III

You're now approaching the alien dig site where the artifact is stored. At the end of the short corridor behind you is another lift. Jump onto it (to avoid falling into the space between the catwalk and the lift platform) and take it down to the level below. Eliminate the Izanagi patrolling the bridge.

Don't cross the bridge right away. Collect the ammo and health lying on and below the platform before you move on. As you gather up the goodies, watch out for the two Auto Turrets hidden under the bridge below the outer security hatch (see figure 15-9). If you manage to eliminate the turrets, you can charge your shield at the energy station on the platform behind them.

Fig. 15-9. Two Auto Turrets hidden under the bridge outside the alien complex protect the ammo that's stored here.

When you're ready, cross the bridge and open the security hatch to enter the alien complex.

When you step inside, you're in a curved corridor that leads left or right. Turn right and follow the corridor, eliminating any Izanagi you encounter. When you get to a door on your right, go through. Follow the corridor through the next door.

There's a metal platform in the room beyond. Kill the Izanagi stationed there, and climb a series of ladders until you reach the corridor at the top. At the other end of the corridor, you overhear a pair of Izanagi discussing what sounds like a dangerous situation ahead. Jump across to the platform in front of you. If you can see the Izanagi below, pop them from the platform. If not, climb down the ladder and take them out downstairs.

The corridor below, which curves off to the left and right, is blocked by lasers that inflict a rather painful zap if you walk through them (see figure 15-10). Only a few beams are immediately apparent, but as you proceed more activate to block your way.

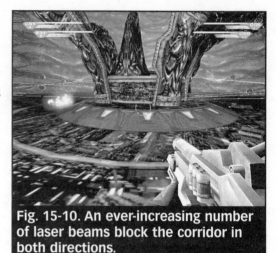

Fig. 15-10. An ever-increasing number of laser beams block the corridor in both directions.

The only way to get past the lasers is to duck and jump your way through the maze. You can take a few hits along the way, but don't take too many—you need your health for the battle ahead. If you get caught in a beam, move away from it immediately. The longer you're exposed, the more damage you take.

When you get to the opposite side of the central hub, you see a pedestal that holds the artifact you're looking for. Step onto the pedestal and take it.

Moments later, all hell breaks loose. In a cutscene, you see a group of Izanagi get slaughtered by a Drakk. Moments later, the security lasers disappear and the central column opens up. A Medium Drakk rises from the column and starts attacking you.

How you deal with the creature is up to you. One way is to run and dodge while blasting the Medium Drakk with everything you've got. However, if you still have the Takkras and the Auto Turret you picked up earlier in the mission, there's an easier way.

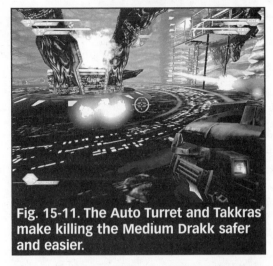

Fig. 15-11. The Auto Turret and Takkras make killing the Medium Drakk safer and easier.

Set up the Auto Turret so that it faces the Drakk, and then launch the Takkras at the creature. The automated devices do the lion's share of the work while you stand back out of harm's way (see figure 15-11).

After the Medium Drakk is dead, retrace your steps up the ladder and into the corridor. Keep your eyes and ears open for Drakk, which are now roaming all over the complex (see figure 15-12).

Continue retracing your steps until you reach the inner security hatch. Step through the door to end the mission.

Fig. 15-12. After you take the artifact, the entire complex swarms with Drakk.

Back on the *Atlantis*

After the cutscene, go to the briefing room where Aida is waiting. After you get the lowdown on the next mission, you can converse with Aida about a number of topics (although it's not required).

Isaak gives a briefing on the Takkra and information on a new weapon he put together from Drakk pieces (the Drakk Laser Rifle). After you assimilate the weapon info, go to the drop room and launch the next mission.

Chapter 16: NC962VIII (Drakk Hive Planet)

The seventh and final artifact is located on NC962VIII, a planet thought to be the homeworld of the Drakk—the nasty robotic creatures you fought on Na-Koja Abad. Everyone in your crew has reservations about this mission, but you head off to finish the job you started.

Mission Objectives:

- ENTER THE DRAKK HOMEWORLD.
- SECURE THE LAST REMAINING ARTIFACT.
- DISCOVER WHAT HAPPENED TO PREVIOUS VISITORS.
- FIND OUT WHY THE DRAKK ARE COLLECTING LIVING SPECIMENS.
- DESTROY THE DRAKK OVERSEERS TO OPEN THE DOORS.
- FIND OUT WHAT THE DRAKK ARE DOING WITH THE LIVING BODY PARTS.
- FIND OUT WHAT THE DRAKK COULD POSSIBLY WANT TO ACHIEVE WITH THEIR EXPERIMENTS.
- RIDE THE GRAVITY LIFT TO THE CENTER OF THE DRAKK STRUCTURE.
- FIND A WAY INTO THE HEART OF THE DRAKK.
- DEFEAT THE DRAKK CARETAKER.

Part I: Suspicion

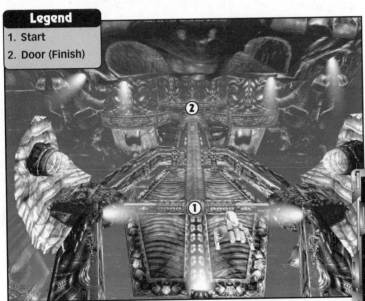

Legend
1. Start
2. Door (Finish)

Fig. 16-1. NC962VIII map, part I

This part of the mission is simple. From the drop ship, take the path directly in front of you to the front door. Walk in for the next part of the mission.

Caution

When you run around outside the complex, avoid the walkway edges. It's a long way to the ground.

Part II: Scrutiny

Legend	
1. Start	5. Chasm Jump
2. Drakk Droid Station	6. Corridors to "Strange Buttons"
3. Shaft	7. Airshaft to Upper Level
4. Forcefields	8. Finish (Upper Level)

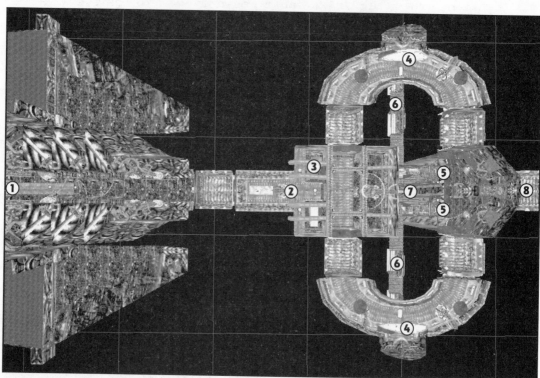

Fig. 16-2. NC962VIII map, part II

When you pass through the inner door, some Drakk appear at the opposite end of the corridor. Eliminate them and proceed forward. Gather ammunition and health from the stockpiles on either side of the corridor, and go through the next two doors.

Just beyond the Drakk Droid station, you encounter more resistance. Eliminate the attacking Drakk and enter the large room beyond.

Fig. 16-3. Explore the shaft next to the entry ramp before you try the doors leading out of the large room.

The room has two exits—one left, one right—but ignore them for the moment. On your left as you descend the ramp into the center of the room is a shaft with stair-like platforms leading into it (see figure 16-3). Drop down into the shaft from step to step. Look around for an opening in the wall. Jump to the step in front of the opening and enter the corridor beyond.

Move to the end of the corridor in a crouch to avoid the steam discharge on the walls. The goal: two Drakk Laser Rifle pods. It may seem like a lot of work for a little ammo, but these clips are scarce and the Drakk Laser Rifle is one of the best weapons on this level.

Retrace your steps to the shaft, and use the platforms to jump back to the room above.

Both exits ultimately lead to the same place, so the choice is yours. Traverse the corridors beyond the exits, eliminating all Drakk along the way. When you reach the door at the end of the corridor, you overlook a chasm. The platform below contains a Drakk Droid station. Eliminate any Drakk resistance and drop down to the platform (see figure 16-4).

Caution

Be careful when descending into the shaft. Falling to the bottom means certain death.

Fig. 16-4. The platform below is your destination. Get a running start and drop onto it.

Enter the right corridor that leads off the platform. Proceed to the T-junction at the end of the corridor. Check for Drakk in both directions and eliminate them.

The right passage leads to a "strange button" that is blocked by several lasers (see figure 16-5). Jump and duck to the button and press it.

Fig. 16-5. Proceed through the lasers and press the button at the end of the right corridor.

Retrace your steps to the T-junction. (The lasers are deactivated now, so the path is safe.) Past the junction, you reach an airshaft. Get a running start and move through the airshaft. Your momentum should carry you past the swirling column to the corridor on the other side. Follow the corridor to the end and press the other "strange button" you find there.

Turn around and head back to the airshaft. This time, step into the swirling column. The column lifts you upward to the level above. When you see the upper opening, step through it. Don't worry if you miss on the first try—the swirling column continues to bounce you back up until you get it right.

It doesn't matter which of the two openings you step through on the upper level—both lead to the same destination. Follow the corridor onto a large platform. Cross the narrow bridge and exit through the door on the other side to proceed to the mission's next phase.

Part III: Subjugation

Legend
1. Start
2. "Chamber of Horrors"
3. Drakk Hatches
4. Experimentation Chamber
5. Airshaft to Next Section (Finish)

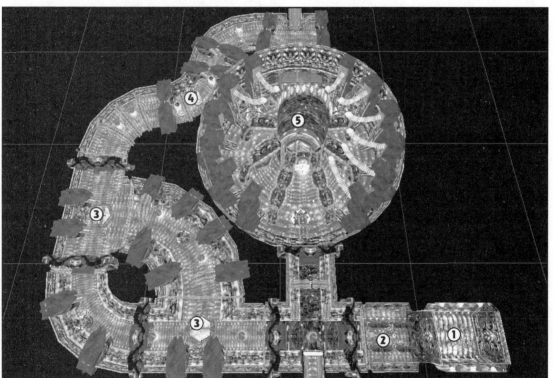

Fig. 16-6. NC962VIII map, part III

Move through the door into the chamber of horrors beyond and stock up on ammo. Proceed through the corridor to the T-junction and continue straight through into the chamber beyond. Just ahead is a hexagonal hatch in the floor. As soon as you step inside the chamber, the hatch opens and a Drakk rises from it (see figure 16-7). Blast the Drakk and continue through the oval opening across the room and into the corridor.

Fig. 16-7. Any time you encounter a hexagonal "Drakk hatch" in the floor, expect a Drakk to rise from it.

Caution

Don't step too close to a Drakk hatch when it's open. If you fall in, the hatch closes behind you and you can't get out.

Continue moving straight into the next chamber (with another Drakk hatch to contend with) and into the corridor beyond. Expect more Drakk resistance along the way. Following a straight path eventually leads you to another experimentation chamber. Stock up on ammo, health, and energy, and continue forward through the chamber and into the corridor beyond.

The corridor terminates in a large chamber with several hexagonal Drakk hatches surrounding a central pillar (see figure 16-8). This time, the hatches don't open—the Drakk are already hiding throughout the chamber.

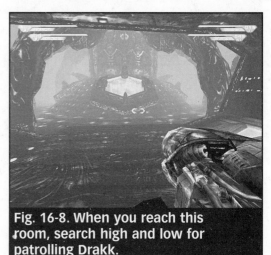

Fig. 16-8. When you reach this room, search high and low for patrolling Drakk.

After you kill the Drakk, a cutscene shows an opening appearing in the central pillar. Inside the opening is an airshaft like the one you rode in the last section of this level. Step through the opening and into the swirling column to proceed to Part IV.

Caution

When you step into the airshaft, stay near the middle of the room. Otherwise you hit the ceiling above and come crashing down to the floor.

Part IV: Subordination

Legend	
1. Start	4. Entrance to Laser Corridor (Lower Level)
2. Drakk Hatches	5. Torture Cage
3. Entrance to Ammo Corridor (Lower Level)	6. Ramp to Central Pillar Exit (Finish)

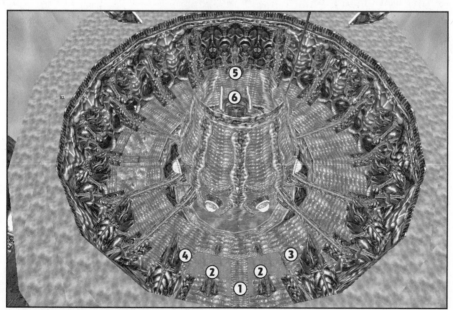

Fig. 16-9. NC962VIII map, part IV

The first chamber contains a Drakk hatch off to your left. When the Drakk pops out, blast it. Proceed through the doorway directly ahead. The door closes behind you as soon as you step through, so there's no turning back.

Head down the ramp and turn right. Eliminate the Drakk when it rises from the hatch there and enter the short corridor beyond. Pick up the ammo and double back to the base of the ramp. Move past the ramp, blast the other Drakk when it pops up, and move to the opening of the corridor beyond.

This corridor is blocked by a cascading series of laser traps (see figure 16-10). Note the timing of the lasers, and run through the corridor when the path is clear. There's no safe place to pause along the way, and ducking and jumping don't help. Time your run so you pass through each corridor segment when the path ahead is clear.

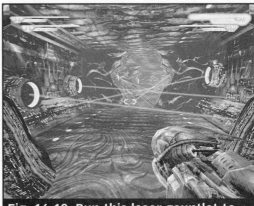

Fig. 16-10. Run this laser gauntlet to proceed.

On the other end of the laser corridor, ascend the ramp, turn around, and proceed onto the central platform. Turn left and follow the platform until you come to a glass cage housing a mutated human.

Note

Two controls outside the glass cage allow you to torture the mutant inside (see figure 16-11). Press the green "sinister orb" to release the subject from its restraints, and press the orange one to zap the subject with electricity while it runs around. After it's zapped a couple of times, the mutant breaks out of the cage and attacks you. Torturing this poor wretch is optional and not required to continue to the next section of the level.

Stock up on the health, energy, and ammo lying around the glass cage, and then proceed up the ramp directly opposite the cage to the door in the central pillar. Step through the door to proceed to the next part of the mission.

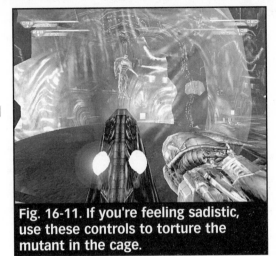

Fig. 16-11. If you're feeling sadistic, use these controls to torture the mutant in the cage.

Part V: Solitude

Legend
1. Start
2. Drakk Boss Hatch
3. Artifact

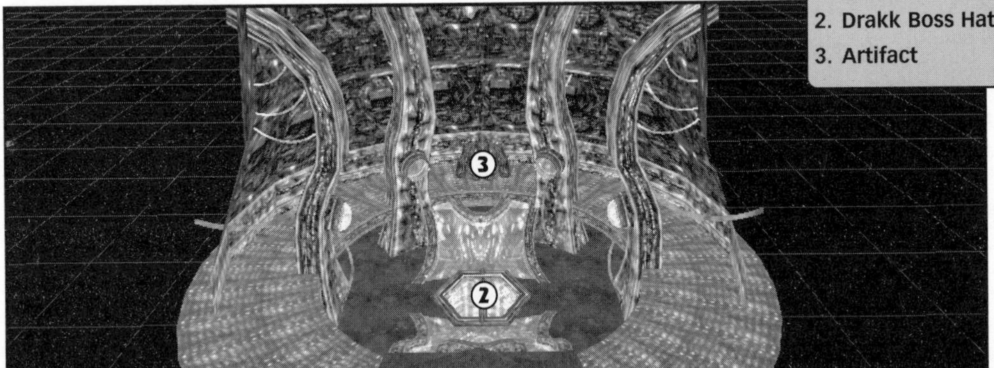

Fig. 16-12. NC962VIII map, part V

Step through the door into the chamber beyond. The cutscene that plays next shows you everything that's about to happen. Note the position of the glass orb with the green glow inside, but focus most of your attention on the Drakk Boss rising from the floor hatch. When the cutscene ends, the Drakk blasts you (see figure 16-13).

Fig. 16-13. The Drakk Boss rises from its hatch in the cutscene and blasts when you're in control.

Note

For details on the Drakk Boss's abilities and characteristics, see Chapter 4.

Start moving and don't stop! Descend the ramp to the floor below and fight from there. Take cover behind the columns that support the upper catwalk. There's ammo, health, and energy behind these columns.

EMP Grenades make great weapons against the Drakk Boss. You need a direct hit to inflict damage, so you must be close (or you have to arc the grenade perfectly). Wait until the Drakk lines up a shot, move in close, and blast it at point-blank range (see figure 16-14).

Fig. 16-14. If you can score a direct hit, EMP Grenades are very effective against the Drakk Boss.

When the Drakk Boss splits, you're halfway through the battle. You must pursue one section of the creature at a time. To destroy the Drakk Boss, destroy its lower half first. If given enough time, the bottom half of the Drakk Boss generates a new top half. You must prevent this from happening to end the battle in a timely manner—and escape with your life! If you attack the top half first, you'll find yourself facing a fully-regenerated Drakk Boss when you turn around.

Caution

After the Drakk Boss splits into two parts, watch your back. Make sure one half doesn't ambush you while you blast the other.

When you deliver the death shot to the Drakk's second half, it spins in place and builds up to an overload. Move away from it quickly! When it explodes, the glass orb on the upper catwalk shatters. Step into the green glow to retrieve the last artifact and end the mission.

Back on the *Atlantis*

Aida informs you that the *Atlantis* is bound for Avalon. There's no briefing this time, but Isaak has some information on the new alt-fire feature on the Drakk Laser Rifle that you might find interesting.

Go to the drop room and head to Avalon.

Chapter 17: Avalon

The *Atlantis* has reached Avalon, and it looks as if your mission is nearing completion. Leaving the artifacts aboard the *Atlantis*, you head down to Avalon to discuss the situation with Drexler and the marines. Unfortunately, things are not exactly as they seem….

Mission Objectives:

- DISCOVER WHAT SHOT YOU DOWN.
- GET UP TO THE CONTROL TOWER.
- DISABLE THE PLANETARY CANNON.
- MEET UP WITH MCMILLAN AT THE LANDING PAD.
- PROTECT THE MARINE TECHNICIAN WHILE HE FIXES THE BACKUP GENERATOR.
- DEFEND THE AREA UNTIL THE *ATLANTIS* CAN ARRIVE.

Avalon

As you descend to Avalon, the planetary cannon opens fire on your drop ship. The ship is damaged and you crash-land near TCA Headquarters. Aida informs you that the marines are nowhere to be found and that the Skaarj have taken over the building and are in control of the planetary cannon. Apparently, you've walked into a trap!

Fig. 17-2. Use the boulder for cover while dealing with the first Skaarj.

The drop ship is wrecked. You have to disable the cannon so that the *Atlantis* can land and retrieve you.

Start toward the building, following the path along the face of the hill to your left. When you can go no farther, step off of the rock and drop down onto the ground below. When you hear a Skaarj approaching from the direction of the base, take cover behind the large boulder and blast it from long range (see figure 17-2).

Caution

All ammo is in very limited supply in this mission, so conservation is important. Sniper Rifle ammo is particularly critical. *Don't use your Sniper Rifle before you shut down the planetary cannon.* You need all the Sniper Rifle ammo you can get later in the mission.

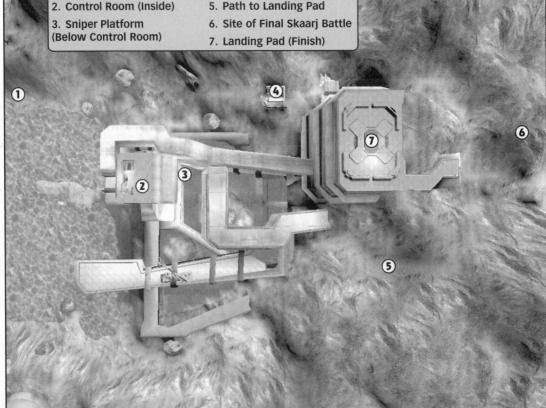

Legend

1. Start
2. Control Room (Inside)
3. Sniper Platform (Below Control Room)
4. Power Generator
5. Path to Landing Pad
6. Site of Final Skaarj Battle
7. Landing Pad (Finish)

Fig. 17-1. Avalon map

Head up the hill toward the building. Watch your left flank as you crest the hill—a Skaarj ambush awaits. There's no cover here, so keep moving and try to maintain some distance between you and the Skaarj during the fight. Additional Skaarj arrive on the scene when you reach the concrete walkway under the building. Wipe them out to continue.

Head toward the central pillar of the nearest part of the structure. Climb the stairs and ride the elevator to the top. When you exit the car, clear the catwalk of Skaarj (they're usually to your right). Turn left and grab the Sniper Rifle ammo on the platform there (taking care not to fall over the edge), and then climb the stairs at the opposite end of the catwalk.

Fig. 17-3. The control room is manned by multiple Skaarj.

When you reach the platform above, expect another Skaarj encounter. Go up the steps to the control room when the coast is clear. Take a quick look through the control room window to assess the situation. Inside, multiple Skaarj (including a Medium one) man the controls (see figure 17-3).

Retreat down the stairs to the first landing. After the planetary cannon fires, one of the Skaarj comes out to patrol the stairway. Eliminate it and stand your ground, a heavy weapon at the ready (the Rocket Launcher is a good choice). Moments later, the first Skaarj's heavier companion exits the control room. Blast it, climb the stairs, and enter the room, which is clear of resistance. Stock up on ammo, health, and energy, then deactivate the planetary cannon from the central control station.

Once the cannon is out of commission, Aida informs you that a marine squad is holed up in the building near the landing pad. You now must reach that location so that the *Atlantis* can pick you up.

Retrace your steps to the elevator and press the control button. The Skaarj have cut the power, so the elevator doesn't work. The marines send out a volunteer to fix the generator, but you have to cover him. Arm yourself with the Sniper Rifle and head over to the sniper platform that overlooks the generator (to your left as you exit the elevator). Engage the scope and keep your eyes open for Skaarj as the marine fixes the generator (see figure 17-4).

Fig. 17-4. Keep a close eye on the marine and snipe every Skaarj that comes along.

The first Skaarj come in from the hills while the marine is still outside the generator fence. After he blows the fence and goes inside, more Skaarj arrive, from both the hills and the area under the base structure. After these are eliminated, Skaarj start arriving from every direction. Most are the Light variety, but there are a few Medium Skaarj thrown in to make things interesting.

Take out the Skaarj as quickly as you can, keeping them as far away from the marine as possible. Shoot as many as you can when you first spot them, and then focus on the opening in the fence. The Skaarj tend to bunch up in the opening because it's the only way in.

If the marine dies, the mission ends in failure. Make every shot count—there's no way to accurately hit the Skaarj from this range with any weapon other than the Sniper Rifle.

Tip

Several explosive cylinders are scattered around both inside the generator fence and outside to either side of the entrance. Shoot them when multiple Skaarj are nearby to take out several enemies with a single shot.

When the marine completes his task, ride the elevator to the ground floor. Follow the marine and stick close to him so that you can help each other deal with the many Skaarj you encounter along the way. Most of the resistance comes from the far end of the walkway. Try to take out the Skaarj at long range—they're a lot harder to deal with up close.

You meet several waves of Skaarj on your way to the landing pad, and they come in all varieties. The first couple of waves come from ahead and to the left, the third comes from the hills on the right, and the fourth—which includes a Heavy Skaarj—comes from the left, near the top of the hill.

Tip

You're likely to lose your marine escort in one of the many Skaarj ambushes on the way to the landing pad. You can still get there without his help. To get to the landing pad from the elevator, turn right, then left along the concrete walkway. Follow the walkway to the end and up the dirt path into the hills beyond. Follow the path into the hills, then turn left at the top to get to the landing pad (see figure 17-5).

Fig. 17-5. Looking back along the path you must follow from the elevator to the landing pad

When you reach the landing pad, the marines introduce themselves and Aida announces that she's on the way. Unfortunately, so are more Skaarj. The marines set up a perimeter, but the Skaarj break through in no time (see figure 17-6). Use whatever means you have left to fight off the attack.

Fig. 17-6. The marine perimeter doesn't hold back the Skaarj for long.

A second wave of Skaarj arrives immediately after the first is eradicated. The enemies arrive from the top of the hill in the distance and proceed through the valley on the left. Once again, use whatever means possible to fend off the attack.

Aida beams you a mysterious transmission. When you kill the last Skaarj, the *Atlantis* comes into view but is shot down short of the landing pad. The marine leader, McMillan, calls for evacuation by Hawkins's flagship, the *Dorian Gray*, and the mission ends.

Chapter 18: *Dorian Gray*

Aboard the *Dorian Gray*, Hawkins informs you that there were no survivors when the *Atlantis* was destroyed. The wreckage was searched and the artifacts were brought aboard the *Dorian Gray*. The glyphs show that an ancient race, the Tosc, hid their DNA in another race—the Kai! It is believed that assembling the artifacts will revert the Kai to their Tosc form.

Hawkins intends to assemble the artifacts in the hopes that the Tosc will use their weapons to serve him in the war against the Skaarj. You and your marine companions stand watch in case something happens.

Mission Objectives:

- FIND A WAY TO PLAY BACK AIDA'S BURST TRANSMISSION.
- KILL THE TOSC.
- FIND THE SECTOR COMMANDER.
- FIND A WAY TO PLAY BACK AIDA'S BURST TRANSMISSION.
- KILL THE TOSC.
- FIND THE SECTOR COMMANDER.

- GET TO THE ESCAPE PODS.
- USE THE FAILING GRAVITY TO GET TO THE UPPER LEVELS.
- FIND AN UNUSED ESCAPE POD BEFORE THE SHIP IS DESTROYED.

Part I: The Vault

Legend
1. Start
2. Containment Field Area
3. Health and Energy Stations
4. Exit Bulkhead
5. Control Room
6. Holo-Message Room (Finish)

Fig. 18-1. Dorian Gray map, part I

While Hawkins makes his speech, run around the room and gather all of the weapons and ammo you can find in the alcoves around the room.

When Hawkins assembles the artifacts, the Kai in the containment field grows to massive proportions and attacks everything in sight (see figure 18-2). Keep moving and blast it with all you've got. Try to keep a column or girder between you and the creature. The Singularity Cannon (the Tosc's primary weapon) inflicts damage by pulling you toward the singularity it creates. If you're wedged behind a column, the weapon can't draw you in.

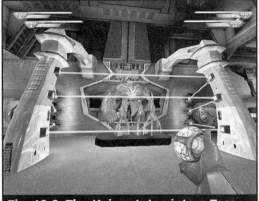

Fig. 18-2. The Kai mutates into a Tosc when Hawkins assembles the artifacts.

The marines help draw fire away from you at first, but they don't last long. Keep blasting away at the creature, especially when it's occupied with the marines.

After you inflict damage, the Tosc drops its Singularity Cannon. Pick up the weapon—it works better against the creature than anything your carry.

When the creature is destroyed, stock up on health, energy, and ammo in the room opposite the containment field area. (The bulkheads that lead there open up when the Tosc is killed.) Exit the room through the bulkhead to the left of the containment field area. Follow the corridor to the first door on the left and enter the room beyond. Once inside, a cutscene shows the message Aida downloaded to you before the _Atlantis_ was destroyed. It reveals that Hawkins has been manipulating you all along!

As the message ends, you hear Hawkins's voice beyond the far bulkhead, and the next part of the mission begins.

Part II: The *Dorian Gray*

Legend	
1. Start	5. Engine Room Upper Walkway
2. Control Room	6. Unpredictable Gravity Begins
3. Engine Room	7. Escape Pod (Finish)
4. Engine Room Catwalks	

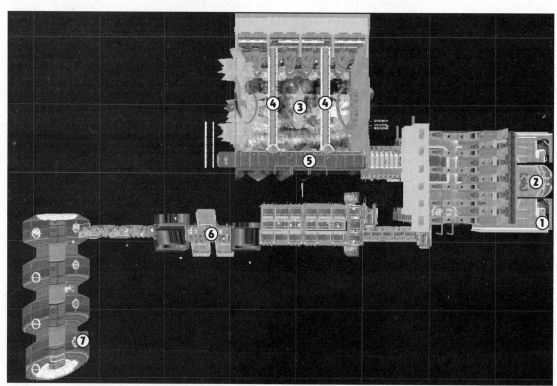

Fig. 18-3. Dorian Gray map, part II

Exit the room and go up the ramp to the control room. When you reach Hawkins's position, he tells you his plan and asks you to join him. You kill him and set course for the star to destroy the *Dorian Gray* and all of the Tosc aboard. Now you must exit the ship before it's destroyed!

Exit the bridge through the bulkhead behind you. In the room beyond, another Tosc is on the rampage. Deal with it and exit the room through the door on the other side.

Proceed through the corridor and into the engine room. The marines here are dealing with another Tosc onslaught. Stock up on health and energy if you need it, and turn right onto the catwalk that spans the room. Don't to fall into the deadly liquid. Watch the marines on the left catwalk to determine the location of the Tosc. Cross the catwalk and fight from the ledge on the other side (see figure 18-4). Use the columns between you and the enemy to protect you from the Singularity Cannon blasts.

Fig. 18-4. Fight the Tosc in the engine room from the ledge, using the columns as cover.

Caution

Avoid the walkway's open edge. Otherwise, Singularity Cannon blasts can pull you out over the abyss and cause you to fall into the deadly liquid below.

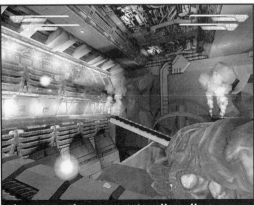

Fig. 18-5. The rear catwalk collapses during the battle and causes the gravity partially to fail.

During the battle, the second catwalk collapses and the gravity engine fails (see figure 18-5). With the gravity reduced, you can make it to the upper walkway.

After the threat is eliminated, move down the ledge to the end of the broken catwalk and step onto it. Get a running start and jump across to the slanted section on the other side. Starting at the bottom of the slanted section, get a running start (see figure 18-6), and jump toward the small ledge just right of the balcony above. Once on the ledge, face the balcony, back up as far as you can, and take a running leap onto the balcony.

Fig. 18-6. Get a running start from the bottom of the broken catwalk and jump to the ledge to the right of the balcony.

Follow the upper walkway to the bulkhead door at the front end of the room and go through. Continue forward through the next door and into the cargo bay beyond. When you enter, the door on the other side of the room seals. Gather some health, energy, and equipment in the storeroom (behind the only bulkhead on this level that opens) and prepare to make another jump.

Above you are two balconies, each with a door leading off it. One of the door control panels is red (meaning it's sealed). The other is green. Position yourself on the catwalk so you face the balcony holding the unsealed door (see figure 18-7). Take a running leap onto the platform and go through the door.

Fig. 18-7. Line yourself up with the balcony leading to the unlocked bulkhead and jump to it.

Turn right through the first bulkhead door, and move forward until you reach a large bay where a pair of marines is babbling about getting to the escape pods. Proceed through either bulkhead door. There's a Tosc in the room beyond, so prepare for battle. When the Tosc is dead, jump to the left catwalk above and continue forward (in the direction you were originally headed).

When you reach the bulkhead door at the end of the catwalk, the ship starts listing. Your perspective is tilted and gravity shifts (see figure 18-8).

Fig. 18-8. The ship's situation worsens as you head toward the escape pods.

Proceed through the door at the end of the corridor, and through the next two bulkhead doors beyond that. When you reach a round room with a long central shaft, your trek through the ship is almost complete. Deal with one final Tosc here.

Tip

The final dash to the escape pod is disorienting and difficult. You have 30 seconds to reach the pod and launch after you destroy the final Tosc. Save the game before you kill the final Tosc.

After the Tosc dies, follow the central shaft to the top, where a remaining escape pod waits (see figure 18-9). You have 30 seconds to reach the pod before the ship is destroyed. When you reach the pod, step up to it and press the "use" control to end the mission.

Fig. 18-9. This escape hatch is your final destination.

Epilogue

As the escape pod departs, you hear Aida, Isaak, and Ne'Ban's last words to you, praising your actions and wishing you well. You fly off into the great unknown to contemplate your bittersweet victory.

Part III: Appendix

Cheat Codes and Easter Eggs

In this section, we reveal the built-in cheats and easter eggs that the developers put in the game.

Cheat Codes

Unreal II–The Awakening includes a number of cheat codes to make things easier when the going gets tough. To enable the cheats, press ~ and type BEMYMONKEY.

Once the cheats are enabled, type the codes as shown, and press enter . Press esc to return to the game. (After the cheats are enabled, you can enter new cheats by simply pressing ~, entering the desired code, and pressing enter .)

- **ALLAMMO**: This gives you the maximum amount of ammunition for all of the weapons you are currently carrying.

- **FLY**: Nullifies gravity allowing you to move through the air as if you were walking. This comes in handy when you are having trouble "legally" making a jump.

- **GHOST**: This cheat allows you to walk through walls, ceilings, floors, and other solid objects.

Caution

The GHOST cheat actually allows you to leave the map. Odd, unpredictable things can happen when you exit the confines of the level.

- **GOD**: Makes you virtually indestructible. You are immune to weapon and fall damage, but you are subject to damage effects from fire.

Caution

You must re-enter the GOD cheat every time a new section of the level loads.

- **GOODIES 0 100**: Enter this to gain all of the weapons in the game, as well as one each of the following: Auto Turret, Rocket Turret, Plasma Field Generator, and Proximity Sensor.

- **INVISIBLE (1/0)**: INVISIBLE 1 makes you invisible to all enemies, traps, doors, and so on. INVISIBLE 0 make you visible again.

- **OPEN *mapname***: Allows you to open any *Unreal II* map, where *mapname* is the name of the map you want to open. The maps for all of the game levels are located in the *Maps* folder. You must type the file extension as well as the name. (Example: OPEN *M11.un2*.)

- **PHOENIX**: When this cheat is enabled, you are instantly resurrected with full health and shields when you die.

- **PLAYERSONLY**: When this cheat is enabled, the entire game world is frozen. Nothing moves except for you. Entering PLAYERSONLY again restarts the action.

- **SLOMO *speed***: Controls the speed of the game. 1 is the default normal speed. Entering a number lower than 1 (example: SLOMO 1) causes the action to proceed in slow motion. Zero (0) is the slowest possible speed. Entering a number higher than 1 causes the action to proceed in fast motion.

- **TOGGLERELOADS**: When this cheat is active, you don't have to reload your weapon—you can continue firing without interruption until all of your ammo is exhausted.

- **WALK**: This code nullifies the effects of the FLY and GHOST cheats. When you enter this, make sure you're not in the middle of space, outside the defined map boundaries, or hundreds of feet above the map floor to avoid unpredictable—or deadly—results.

Easter Eggs

The developers at Legend Entertainment included fun hidden features in the game. The following sections provide a guide to the location and function of these easter eggs.

Avalon (Training Mission)

- **Secret Nali Shooting Range:** When you mantle onto the raised block in the obstacle course, jump over the fence on the right. Step inside the crate to pick up the head. Proceed with the rest of the course and let Raff run you through the three weapons on the shooting range. When Raff finishes the weapons training, proceed to the fourth shooting range (the one beyond the Grenade Launcher range). The range gate opens, revealing a pair of Nali targets you can blast to your heart's content.

Aboard the Atlantis

There are a number of easter eggs aboard the *Atlantis*. The following are available during any *Atlantis* interlude:

- **Seagoat Hologram:** In the briefing room, there's a hidden button on the holotank's right side, on the table's edge in the small space between the table and the wall. When you press it, a hologram of a Seagoat appears in the holotank.

- **Flashbang:** In the Armory, there is a secret button located inside the door (under the edge of Isaak's computer station). When you press this button, you hear Isaak say "Flashbang!", and an EMP blast goes off.

- **A Few Laughs:** Follow the upper corridor toward the back of the ship, past Ne'Ban's quarters, and jump into the open hatch. Turn toward the front of the ship to see a tiny hidden button inside (on the left, near the top). When you press this button, Lincoln and Grant appear and laugh at you.

- **License Plate:** You must use the "Ghost" cheat for this one. Go behind the locker in John's quarters to see a Virginia license plate that says "Seagoat" attached to the back of the locker.

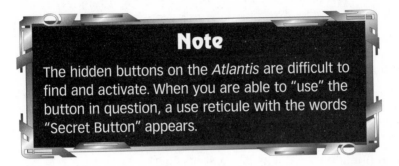

Note

The hidden buttons on the *Atlantis* are difficult to find and activate. When you are able to "use" the button in question, a use reticule with the words "Secret Button" appears.

A number of additional easter eggs appear aboard the *Atlantis* as the game progresses:

- **Dalton's "Photo Album":** After each completed mission, a new photograph of the planet you just visited is attached to the large screen in John's cabin.

- **Artifacts:** Whenever you find a piece of the alien artifact during a mission, it appears on the table in the back of the Armory during the succeeding interludes.

- **Wandering Seagoat:** During all *Atlantis* interludes after the Kalydon mission, there is a Seagoat aboard the *Atlantis*. If you find it, it runs away the first two times. Thereafter, you can interact with it and hear Dalton make a comment about it.

Finally, there are several *Atlantis* easter eggs that are specific to certain *Atlantis* Interludes:

- **First Interlude:** During the first *Atlantis* Interlude (number 2 on the Missions menu), you can activate a special version of the mission briefing. Open the hatch on the upper deck opposite Ne'Ban's quarters and interact with the Seagoat inside. Reply to the Seagoat as follows: "Spam," "Spam," "Spam," "Humbug." You receive a message that "Lincoln is pleased." Proceed to Aida's briefing. During the briefing, Abraham Lincoln appears on the briefing screen instead of Danny Miller when Aida plays the distress call.

- **Fifth Interlude:** (Number 11 on the Missions menu.) When Ne'Ban gives the mission briefing for the Kalydon mission, 12 images display in the holotank in rapid succession. Use the "Slomo" cheat to get a good look at the images.

Secret Interludes

There are two secret *Atlantis* Interludes you can access from the console by pressing ⬚ and typing the appropriate command:

- **_Unreal II_ Dance Party:** At any time, open the console and type OPEN ATLANTIS?MISSIONCOMPLETED=83, then press ⬚ enter ⬚. You'll find yourself at a Seagoat dance party on the bridge of the *Atlantis*, complete with balloons and a shiny *Unreal* logo.

- **Balloons Aplenty:** At any time, open the console and type OPEN ATLANTIS?MISSIONCOMPLETED=110276, then press ⬚ enter ⬚. You'll find yourself in John's cabin, surrounded by floating Seagoat and Abraham Lincoln balloons. There are additional balloons in the corridor outside.

TIP

To exit the secret interludes, return to the menu and load another mission.

Index

A

air, supply while swimming, 11

ALLAMMO

cheat code, 174

Acheron, 92–97

artifact, 96

enemies

Izanagi Mercenaries, 93–97

health, energy & ammo stores, 95, 96

map, 94

mission objectives, 93

Rocket Turrets, 95

weapons

Frag Grenades, 95

Rocket Launcher, 95

Aida, 32, 72, 133, 145, 157

Atlantis Interlude, 56–58

briefing

Acheron, 91

Hell, 75

Janus, 119

message from Atlantis, 167

mysterious transmission, 164

Allies, 31–34. *See also* individual names

Angels. *See* Liandri "Angel" Mercenaries

Araknids, 35, 39–40

Hell, 80–91

pods, 84–85, 90

artifacts, 91, 104

Acheron, 96

Hell, 91

Janus, 127

Na-Kola Abad, 144

NC962VIII, 157

Sanctuary, 70

Atlantis

Interlude, 55–58

briefings, 58

mission objectives, 56

map, 57

repairs at Kalydon, 105–111

EMP Grenades, 22

   against Drakk Boss, 156

   Janus, 123

   NC962VIII, 156–157

   Severnaya, 99, 103, 104

enemies, 35–47. *See also* individual names

   listing by game level, 35

enemy fire, avoiding, 12

Energy Rifle. *See* Shock Lance

energy stations, 17

equipment, 27–29

explosive cylinders

   Avalon, 162–164

F

Fire

   suggested mapping, 15

Firing range, 54

Flamethrower, 21, 79, 83

FLY

   cheat code, 174

forcefields

   Hell, 78

Fragmentation Grenades (Frag Grenades), 22

   Acheron, 95

   Severnaya, 102

G

getting around, 9

GHOST

   cheat code, 174

Ghost Warriors. *See* Izanagi Mercenaries

GOD

   cheat code, 174

GOODIES 0 100

   cheat code, 175

Grace. *See* Pistol

Grenade Launcher, 21–23

   Sulferon, 114–116

   test firing, 54

grenades, 22

Kalydon, 106–111

Severnaya, 101, 103

Sulferon, 113–114

running, 9–10

S

Sanctuary, 59–70

briefing, 58

enemies

Heavy Skaarj, 70

Izarians, 61–69

Skaarjs, 65–70

explosive tanks, 63

health, energy & ammo stores, 65

mission objectives, 60

Part I: Mining Complex Entrance, 60–63

map, 61

Part II: Mining Complex, 63–65

map, 64

Part III: Power Plant, 66–70

map, 66

weapons

Shock Lances, 61, 63

saving games, 15

Seagoats, 47, 72, 104

Severnaya, 98–104

Auto Turret, 101, 103

enemies

Izanagi Mercenaries, 99–104

forcefields, 103, 104

health, energy & ammo stores, 102

map, 100

mission objectives, 99

return to Atlantis, 104

shortwave detonators, 101, 102, 104

weapons

EMP Grenades, 99, 103, 104

Frag Grenades, 102

Rocket Launcher, 101, 103

Sniper Rifle, 99

shields, 16–17

UNREAL TOURNAMENT 2003

www.unrealtournament2003.com

THE YEAR'S MOST ACCLAIMED SHOOTER.

"…beyond anything you've seen before…it's the new face of futuristic combat"
– PC Gamer

"This is unquestionably the most graphically stunning shooter to date."
– GameSpy

"Unreal Tournament 2003 raises the bar for first-person PC action games."
– Philadelphia Inquirer

"Everyone's favorite shooter just got better"
– FHM

"… UT2003 looks effin' amazing."
– PC Gamer

BEST GRAPHICS, TECHNICAL

IGN.COM EDITORS' CHOICE AWARD

ATARI

MATURE
M
Blood and Gore
Violence
CONTENT RATED BY
ESRB

 DIGITAL XTREME

 EPIC GAMES

 The way it's meant to be played™ nVIDIA

 PC CD ROM